6 / 07

COLUMBIA COUNTY LIBRARY

3 0759 1002 6869 2

The Essentials of Hinduism
A Comprehensive Overview of the World's Oldest Religion

D1235871

DISCARD

294.5 BHA
Bhaskarananda, Swami.
 The essentials of Hinduism

07

Swami Vivekananda

The Essentials of Hinduism

A Comprehensive Overview
of the World's Oldest Religion

by
Swami Bhaskarananda

Viveka Press

Seattle

Columbia County Library
220 E. Main St.
P.O. Box 668
Magnolia, AR 71754-0668

Viveka Press, Seattle 98102
©2002 by The Vedanta Society of Western Washington

All rights reserved. No part of this book may be reproduced or transmitted in any form or by any means, electronic or mechanical, including photocopying, recording, or by any information storage and retrieval system, without the written permission of the Publisher, except where permitted by law.

For more information write to:
The Vedanta Society of Western Washington
2716 Broadway Avenue East, Seattle, WA 98102
Phone: (206) 323-1228
Email: society@vedanta-seattle.org
www.vedanta-seattle.org

1st edition 1994
2nd edition 2002

Printed in Canada

Publisher's Cataloging in Publication
(Prepared by Quality Books Inc.)

Bhaskarananda, Swami
   The Essentials of Hinduism : a comprehensive overview of the world's oldest religion / by Swami Bhaskarananda. -- 2nd ed.
   p. cm.
   Includes bibliographical references and index.
   LCCN: 2001091048
   ISBN 1-884852-04-1

   1. Hinduism.   I. Title.
   BL1202.B494 2002   294.5
                        QBI01-200710

Humbly dedicated to
Swami Vivekananda
who was the first
to make Hinduism known to
North America

The picture on the front cover depicts the Paramahamsa—a mythological swan with the ability to drink the essential part of milk rejecting its watery part. In Hinduism, a Paramahamsa is considered a symbol of a spiritually illumined soul who has experienced the Divine Essence of everything by rejecting the worldly lures of the senses. The goal of Hinduism is to experience this Divinity in everything and every being. Furthermore, it is seen that a Paramahamsa remains in water and yet the water never clings to its feathers. Similarly, a spiritually illumined soul lives in the world, yet is never contaminated by it.

Table of Contents

List of Illustrations and Diagrams

PREFACE TO THE FIRST EDITION

During the past twenty years of my stay in the United States, I have been invited to speak on Hinduism at many schools, colleges, and universities. I have also spoken at numerous churches and synagogues. The audiences, for the most part, have had either Christian or Jewish backgrounds, and I have often received requests from these groups to recommend a book which would help them understand Hinduism without having to go through a lot of technical details. Many have complained that the authors of the available books on Hinduism assume that the readers already know quite a bit about the subject, making their presentation difficult for a newly interested reader to understand. Moreover, the descendents of Hindu immigrants, unfamiliar with their religious heritage, ask their parents many questions which they are often unable to answer. Some of these parents requested me to write a book on Hinduism which would address these questions.

These are the reasons which inspired me to write this book. I have tried to make it easy to understand, without indulging in oversimplification. The topics covered address the questions I have most often encountered from western audiences over the last two decades. Keeping in mind that a large volume may easily daunt a college or high school student, the number of pages in this book has been kept well restrained without sacrificing the academic need of the students. An attempt also has been made to make this book helpful to high school and college teachers who cover Hinduism in their classes.

In the publication of this book the following persons

have helped immensely and I acknowledge their loving assistance with deep gratitude.

- Swami Atmatattwananda of the Vedanta Society of Southern California for his help and guidance during the final stages of editing the manuscript.
- Biswa Ranjan Chakraborty of Calcutta for providing various illustrations and the original design upon which the cover is based.
- Diane Fitzgerald for final proofreading of the manuscript.
- Allen R. Freedman for his assistance with some of the diagrams and charts.
- Devra A. Freedman for her help in editing and also preparing the index.
- David Manning for providing thoughtful and constructive suggestions after reading the manuscript.
- Charles Mathias for his many illustrations and the graphic design of the cover.
- Terri Storseth for editing early copies of the manuscript.
- Kathleen & Timothy Teague for help with some of the illustrations.
- Charles S. Wirth for providing assistance with the typesetting and printing of the manuscript.

I also thankfully acknowledge my debt to the following publishers:

- Advaita Ashrama, Mayavati, India, for permission to use quotations from *Great Women of India*.
- The Ramakrishna-Vivekananda Center of New York for permission to use quotations from *The Gospel of Sri Ramakrishna*.
- The Vedanta Society of Southern California for

permission to use quotations from Swami
Prabhavananda's translation of the *Upanishads*.
- John Benjamins Publishing Company, Philadel-
phia, for permission to quote Walter H. Maurer's
translation of the *Nāsadīya Sūkta* contained in
*Pinnacles of India's Past; Selections from the Rg-
Veda.*

I shall consider my labor well rewarded if the book
proves to be helpful to those for whom it is intended.

Swāmī Bhāskarānanda
October, 1994

PREFACE TO THE SECOND EDITION

In this edition slight changes have been made in the
book to make it more accurate and suitable for the reader.

Swāmī Bhāskarānanda
December, 2001

Pronunciation Guide

Sanskrit and other Indian words have been carefully and consistantly transliterated—according to the chart below—hoping that the correct, or at least close, pronunciation will thus be indicated.

a	is to be pronounced as "o" in come
ā	is to be pronounced as in star
e	is to be pronounced as in bed
i	is to be pronounced as in sit
ī	is to be pronounced as in machine
o	is to be pronounced as in note
u	is to be pronounced as in pull
ū	is to be pronounced as in intrude
ai	is to be pronounced as in aisle
au	is to be pronounced as ow in now
bh	is to be pronounced as in abhor
ch	is to be pronounced as in church
chh	is an aspirated version of "ch"
d	is to be pronounced as th in thus
dh	is to be pronounced as in adhere
g	is to be pronounced as in god
gh	is to be pronounced as in leghorn
kh	is to be pronounced as in inkhorn
p	is to be pronounced as in paternal
ph	is to be pronounced as f in fine
th	is to be pronounced as in thaw
sh	is to be pronounced as in shall

I

HISTORY OF HINDUISM

Hinduism is one of the world's major religions. There are over 856 million Hindus today. Most are in India, but sizable populations also live in Nepal, Mauritius, Fiji, South Africa, Sri Lanka, Guyana, Indonesia (Bali) and a few other countries. Hinduism is, by most estimates, several thousand years old and holds the distinction of being the most ancient of the world's living religions.[1] Its exact age, however, is difficult to determine—although it is known to be older than Jainism, Buddhism, Christianity, and Islam. Some scholars believe that Zoroastrianism, which is also one of the oldest religions in the world, owes its origin to the same scriptural source from which Hinduism has come.[2]

THE ANCESTORS OF THE HINDUS
AND THEIR RELIGION

The ancestors of the Hindus were known as *Āryas*. The English counterpart of the Sanskrit word *Ārya* is Aryan, or Indo-Aryan. The Āryas called their religion *Ārya Dharma*—the religion of the Āryas. The word Hinduism was completely unknown to them. The word *dharma*, in

1. *Information Please Almanac* (Boston: Houghton Mifflin Company, 1993), 411.
2. Jatindra Mohan Chatterji, *Hymns of Atharvan Zarathustra* (Calcutta: The Parsi Zoroastrian Association, 1967).

this context, means religion or religious duties.[3] Sanskrit, which belongs to the Indo-European family of languages, was the language of the Indo-Aryans.

The Aryans also called their religion *Mānava Dharma*, or the Religion of Man, meaning that it was not an exclusive religion of the Aryans, but was meant for the whole of mankind. Another name was *Sanātana Dharma*—The Eternal Religion, illustrating their belief that the religion was based on some eternal truths.

The name Hinduism came much later. One of the neighboring countries, Persia, had a common border with ancient India, which at that time was known as Āryāvarta—the land of the Aryans. This common border between Persia and ancient India was the river Indus, called in Sanskrit, Sindhu. The Persians could not pronounce Sindhu correctly; they pronounced it Hindu. They also called the Aryans, living on the other side of the river Sindhu, Hindus; thus the religion of the Aryans became known as Hinduism.

SUPERSENSUOUS TRUTHS—THE BASIS OF HINDUISM

- Where did the universe come from, and how?
- If there is a Creator, what is He like? What is the relationship between the created and the Creator?
- What happens to us when we die?
- Do we exist after our death?
- Did we exist before our birth?

---

3. The Sanskrit word *dharma* has other meanings such as property or quality.

Such questions have challenged the human mind since the dawn of civilization. Even those with the most intelligent minds have not found definite answers to these questions. Whatever answers they have found are based on mere speculation. But some spiritually illumined saints, with the help of their special *purified* minds, found the answers and have made them known to us. These answers were eventually recorded in books known as scriptures.[4] Scriptures, according to Hinduism, are unique in their ability to reveal truths not knowable by average *impure* minds. The difference between an "impure" and a "pure" mind can be explained by the following analogy.

Ice, water and water vapor—all three are the same chemical substance. Yet they differ greatly in their properties. Relatively speaking, ice has the least freedom among the three; it can hardly move. Water has more freedom; it can easily flow and spread out. Water vapor has the maximum amount of freedom. Not only can it freely spread out in every direction, but being invisible, it is also the most subtle of the three. It can reach where neither ice nor water can ever go.

So also is the human mind. An impure mind, no matter how intelligent, has many limitations. It cannot know anything beyond the domain of sense perception or what lies beyond the world of time and space. It cannot know what is going to happen the next moment or what happened in the distant past. Metaphysical truths, such as the knowledge of the existence of God or the hereafter, are beyond the scope of such a mind. But when that

---

4. The Sanskrit definition, *Ajñātajñāpakam shāstram*, means "What makes the unknown known is a scripture."

same mind is *purified* or transformed through spiritual discipline into an extraordinary mind, it can transcend the barriers of the sense world and reach the outermost frontier of the world of time and space. It can then glimpse what lies beyond the domain of the senses. It gains extraordinary capabilities. It becomes all-knowing; it can know all the events of the past, present and the future. A genuine saint possesses such a *pure* mind. With the help of that mind the saint comes to know the truth about God, the soul, creation, etc. Such truths are called *supersensuous*[5] or metaphysical truths. Hinduism, like the other major religions of the world, is based on such truths discovered by its pure-minded sages.

FOUNDER

Hinduism has the unique distinction of having no known founder. One may wonder how there can be a religion without any founder. The eternal and supersensuous truths discovered by ancient Indian sages are the foundation of Hinduism. These sages preferred to remain anonymous because they realized that these Truths must always have existed, just as the laws of gravitation had already existed when they were discovered by Newton. The sages also realized that these Eternal Truths had come from God, the same source from which everything in creation had come. As the Truths were revealed by God, the sages called them *apaurusheya*—not man-made.

Having no known founder gives Hinduism a certain advantage over other religions. Had it been a religion with a specific founder, it would have been hard for Hin-

---

5. Super: *Latin*, above or beyond. Thus "beyond the senses."

duism to undergo the kind of evolution it has experienced during the past many thousand years. Various saints and Divine Incarnations at different times have appeared on the stage, played their individual roles, and enriched Hinduism with their teachings. By reinterpreting earlier scriptural texts they have made the religion relevant to changed times and people. They also have given validity to the scriptural truths through their own spiritual experiences.

Any ancient religion can be compared to the attic of an old home. Unless the attic is regularly cleaned, it gathers dust and cobwebs and eventually becomes unusable. Similarly, if a religion cannot be updated or cleaned from time to time, it loses its usefulness and cannot relate anymore to changed times and people. But this did not happen to Hinduism. Fortunately, at different periods, many genuine saints born in India have cleansed, reformed and revitalized Hinduism and made it relevant to their times. This would not have been possible had Hinduism had a founder.

II

GOD-REALIZATION

THE INEVITABLE GOAL

Hinduism recognizes four goals of human life:

- *Kāma*—satisfying the desire for sense pleasure
- *Artha*—acquisition of worldly possessions or money
- *Dharma*—observance of religious duties
- *Moksha*—liberation achieved through God-realization[1]

Among these four, kāma is considered the lowest because this urge is common to both man and animals. Artha, on the other hand, is noticeable mainly in human beings, and is considered superior to kāma. The third goal, dharma,[2] is no other than a training in self-sacrifice. Kāma and artha are rooted in selfishness, dharma is not. Thus, dharma is superior to kāma and artha.

The Hindu way of life consists in the performance of a series of religious duties or dharma as dictated by the scriptures. Even in order to acquire worldly possessions or to satisfy his passions a Hindu must hold on to dharma. This is why kāma and artha—which are mentioned as

---

1. God-realization means knowing without any doubt that God exists. Such knowledge can only come through directly experiencing God.
2. For more about dharma please see "Dharma or Religious Duties" on page 98.

two separate goals different from dharma—are placed under the category of dharma by some scholars.[3]

Moksha, which means "liberation," can be achieved only through the realization of God. Hinduism believes in God's omnipresence and speaks of the presence of Divinity in every human being. At any given point of time Divinity is equally present in all, but not equally manifest. The purpose of spiritual practice is to manifest this inherent Divinity. When this Divinity becomes fully manifest, a person is said to have become a God-realized soul; he is also said to have attained moksha.

This Divinity is the true Self of man. It forms the very core of man's existence. One can give up whatever is extraneous, but not that which forms the very core of one's being. Sooner or later this true Self, or Divinity, must manifest itself. All without any exception will eventually attain moksha. Some highly evolved souls may accomplish this in this life, or after their death. Others who are not as evolved may need several more incarnations. Conscious effort or sincere spiritual practice, however, can help one to achieve this goal faster. Nonetheless, everybody is unconsciously proceeding towards this goal.

According to Hinduism *Infinite Bliss* is one of the principal aspects of Divinity. Even when man pursues kāma or artha he is unconsciously trying to reach his Divine Self—which is Infinite Bliss.[4] No matter how much plea-

3. D. S. Sharma, *What is Hinduism* (Madras: The Madras Law Journal Press, 1945), 75.

sure or money he gets, he craves for more. He cannot find satisfaction through them, because the joy that he gets from such pleasure or money is finite. Eventually he realizes that searching for Infinite Bliss through such finite external means will lead him nowhere.

This awareness inspires him to turn around and consciously search for that fountain of Infinite Bliss within himself. When he arrives at this perennial source of Infinite Bliss, all his wants and cravings disappear. He then experiences God—the all-pervading Divinity—both within himself and without. He experiences God as the essence of everything and every being. He loves all, even his enemies, because he sees no enemy anywhere. He transcends all suffering, fear and sorrow. In this state any interaction with the world is a most joyous and rewarding experience, because it is no other than directly interacting with God. He sees himself as a part of a Divine play where God is playing all the roles, including his own. He can no longer identify with his body-mind-complex, which is subject to birth, change, decay and death. He gains the unshakable conviction that he is the eternal Divine Spirit—deathless and birthless.

This is moksha or "liberation." Moksha[5] is the inevita-

---

4. Eternity, Perfection, Absolute Knowledge, Absolute Truth, Auspiciousness and Beauty are among the other aspects of God according to Hinduism. These aspects are metaphorical expressions suggesting the indescribable Nirguna Brahman or Impersonal God. To know more about the Hindu concept of Impersonal God, please see page 66.

ble goal of human life. Compared to this intensely bliss-
ful experience every other joy derived from the senses is
tasteless and insipid. The scriptures of Hinduism again
and again urge Hindus to consciously strive for this goal.

---

5. To know more about moksha read the chapter entitled *Moksha or Liberation From Samsāra* on page 179.

III

THE HOLY BOOKS

VEDAS—THE REVEALED TEXTS

The revealed Divine Truths are called the *Vedas*. The Sanskrit word *Veda* means knowledge. The Hindu sages considered these truths so sacred that for a long time they did not put them in writing. They preserved them in their memory and taught them to deserving students through oral instruction.

The sages had phenomenal memory acquired through the practice of celibacy. Celibacy is no other than conservation of energy. The sages of ancient India knew that a person who did not waste his energy through unrestrained sensual pursuits, particularly sexual activity, could greatly enhance his memory and other mental faculties.[1] The other benefits of celibacy were greater longevity and *dhāranā shakti*—the ability to understand the deeper meaning of the scriptures. Equipped with such memory the sages were able to memorize the numerous Vedic Truths. Their students, who were also celibate, heard these Truths, memorized them, and shaped their lives accordingly. As they were learned by hearing and not by reading, the Truths came to be known as *Shruti*, which literally means hearing.

---

1. *Pātanjala Yogasūtra*; Sādhanapāda, Aphorism 38: "Brahmacharyapratishthāyām vīryalābhah"—"By the establishment of continence energy is gained."

11

In the beginning the Aryans were not a unified or homogeneous nation. There were many Aryan tribes. Some of the tribes were fortunate to have sages who had experienced supersensuous Divine Truths. These sages or saints were called *Rishis* or Seers, because they had seen those Truths with their purified minds.

A sage or a saint, in the context of Hinduism, is one who has directly experienced God in this lifetime. A person possessing noble virtues and engaged in doing good deeds is appreciated in Hinduism, but is not necessarily considered a saint. Moreover, Hindu tradition does not recognize sainthood through post-mortem canonization.

In course of time a need was felt to collect and compile the Vedic Truths. A sage named Krishna Dvaipāyana collected them from different sources and recorded them in a book called the *Vedas*. The *Vedas* had four parts—*Rig-Veda, Sāma-Veda, Yajur-Veda* and *Atharva-Veda*.[2] The older texts of the *Vedas*, such as the hymns of the Rig-Veda, are written in an archaic form of Sanskrit called Vedic or, less accurately, Vedic Sanskrit.

In recognition of his monumental compilation of the *Vedas*, Krishna Dvaipāyana was given the name Veda Vyāsa.[3] Hindus still gratefully remember this ancient sage and honor him by celebrating his birthday every year. His birthday is called *Guru Pūrnimā* or Guru's Day. The English counterpart of the Sanskrit word *guru* is teacher.

---

2. According to the *Vishnu Purāna*, Vyāsa was helped by four of his disciples in the compilation of the *Vedas*. Paila helped him to compile the *Rig-Veda*; Vaishampāyana, the *Yajur-Veda*; Jaimini, the *Sāma-Veda*; and Sumantu, the *Atharva-Veda*.
3. The Sanskrit word *vyāsa* means compiler.

In this particular context guru refers to the great teacher Vyāsa.

Krishna Dvaipāyana Vyāsa

The most important message of the *Vedas* is that everything and every being is divine.[4] There are four very important statements in the *Vedas*. They are called *Mahāvākyas* or "great sentences." Three out of these four great sentences speak of the divinity of every soul, the fourth speaks of the nature of God:

---

4. *Sarvam khalv-idam Brahma*—"All, indeed, is Brahman (God)."

- *Aham Brahmāsmi*—I am Brahman (God)
- *Tat tvam asi*—You are That (Brahman)
- *Ayam ātmā Brahma*—This indwelling Self is Brahman
- *Prajnānam Brahma*—Supreme Knowledge is Brahman

Even though God is equally present everywhere He is not equally manifest in every being, every thing or every place. To explain, let us consider four light bulbs of 100 watts each. If turned on, each one will give the same amount of light. Let us now cover the first bulb with one layer of paper, the second with two layers, the third with three layers, and leave the fourth uncovered. When we turn the bulbs on, they will not give the same amount of light. And yet, it cannot be denied that the same amount of light is present in each one. Similarly, God is equally present everywhere, but not equally manifest. His manifestation is greatest in Divine Incarnations and spiritually-illumined souls, and least in a non-living object, such as a rock. Vedic literature asserts the inherently divine nature of man and provides means and methods to manifest this divinity.

According to the estimate of many scholars, the Vedic texts must be at least 4000 years old.[5] There is considerable controversy, however, about when Vyāsa lived, but it must have been before the 4th century B.C. The well-known Hindu grammarian, Pānini, who probably lived in the 4th century B.C., mentions the epic *Mahābhārata* in one of his works. Therefore, Vyāsa, the author of the *Mahābhārata*, most likely lived before the 4th century B.C.

---

5. S. R. Goyal, *A Religious History of Ancient India,* vol. 1 (Meerut, India: Kusumanjali Prakashan, 1984), 49.

Besides the *Vedas*, Hinduism has several other scriptures. But the *Vedas*, being the revealed scriptures, enjoy a special place of honor and are considered the most authentic. The validity of the Vedic texts is never questioned. Their Truths have been repeatedly validated by the experiences of Hindu saints who appeared at different periods of time.

SAMHITĀ AND BRĀHMANA

As mentioned earlier, the *Vedas* have four parts: *Rig-Veda*, *Sāma-Veda*, *Yajur-Veda* and *Atharva-Veda*. Each of these works consists of two sections: *Samhitā* and *Brāhmana*. The former contains hymns, and the latter explains those hymns and instructs how and when to use them.

UPANISHADS

The *Vedas* also contain some highly philosophical portions known as the *Upanishads*. The *Upanishads* are also called *Vedānta*—the acme or culmination of knowledge. Among the 108 Upanishads available today, the following are the most popular: *Isha*, *Kena*, *Katha*, *Mundaka*, *Māndūkya*, *Aitareya*, *Taittirīya*, *Chhāndogya*, *Prashna*, *Shvetāshvatara* and *Brihadāranyaka*.

SMRITIS

All Hindu scriptures, except the *Darshanas* and the *Tantras*, can be placed within two categories: (1) the *Vedas* and (2) the *Smritis*. The Vedic scriptures are the final authority. The scriptures belonging to the smriti category have secondary authority only. All the scriptures, except the *Vedas*, fall under the smriti category.

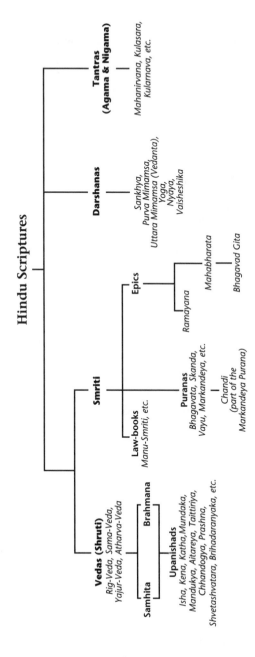

The word *smriti* also has a technical meaning. It means a lawbook[6] or a manual of codes of conduct for the Hindus. Among these ancient lawbooks, the lawbook of Manu is most well known. Yājnavalkya, Baudhāyana, Āpastamba, Vashishtha and Gautama are other ancient law-givers. The latest lawbook was authored by Raghunandana.

DARSHANAS—SCHOOLS OF HINDU RELIGIOUS PHILOSOPHY

Six different systems of philosophy, called *Darshanas*, were developed by Hindu sages at different periods of time. They are "religious" philosophical systems because their foundation is in the *Vedas*. Also known as the Six Systems of Indian Philosophy, they are as follows:

- The *Sānkhya* school founded by Kapila
- The *Pūrva Mīmāmsā* school founded by Jaimini
- The *Uttara Mīmāmsā* or *Vedānta* school founded by Vyāsa
- The *Yoga* school founded by Patanjali
- The *Nyāya* school founded by Gotama
- The *Vaisheshika* school founded by Kanāda

The philosophical system called Vedānta should not be confused with the other meaning of the word, the *Upanishads*.

All the authors of these religio-philosophical systems wrote original treatises using very concise aphorisms, called *sūtras* in Sanskrit. The sūtras, being very brief and terse, needed explanatory notes or commentaries, which

---

6. These lawbooks, authored by the ancient sages of India, are different from the lawbooks pertaining to the legal system of the Indian Government.

were written later by other scholars. Vyāsa's treatise, which forms the basis of the Uttara Mīmāmsā system, is known as *Vedānta Darshana* or *Brahmasūtra*. Several commentaries have been written on this book by famous commentators like Shankarāchārya (c.700–740), Rāmānujāchārya (1017–1137) and Madhvāchārya (1199–1278).

PURĀNAS

The deeper truths of the scriptures of Hinduism are quite difficult and abstruse. They are beyond the scope of most people to understand. The sages of India created a special type of religious literature, called the *Purānas*, in order to present them in an interesting and easily understandable manner. In the Purānas the scriptural teachings are presented through stories and parables. In all, eighteen Purānas are available today, among which *Bhāgavata Purāna, Skanda Purāna, Vāyu Purāna, Padma Purāna, Mārkandeya Purāna* and *Agni Purāna* deserve particular mention. The *Chandī* or *Devīmāhātmyam*, a popular book of Hinduism, is actually a part of the *Mārkandeya Purāna*.

THE TWO EPICS—THE RĀMĀYANA & THE MAHĀBHĀRATA

The Hindus can be proud of two great epics, the *Rāmāyana* and the *Mahābhārata*, which were composed by the sages Vālmīki and Vyāsa respectively. These two epics, which are also called *Itihāsa*, contain many scriptural teachings side by side with the stories of the various Aryan clans and dynasties. They are extremely rich in literary treasures and mythological content. The profusion of moral and spiritual teachings contained in them has raised them to the level of scripture. The *Bhagavad Gītā*, perhaps the most popular scripture of Hinduism, is included in the *Mahābhārata*. Both the *Rāmāyana* and the *Mahābhārata* have many exalted characters who are considered role models by religious-minded Hindus.

THE BHAGAVAD GĪTĀ

This popular Hindu scripture forms a part of the *Mahābhārata*. It contains a dialogue between Shrī Krishna, a Divine Incarnation, and an Aryan prince named Arjuna. In answering the questions of his disciple Arjuna, Shrī Krishna gives many excellent spiritual teachings. These teachings are a great treasure of Hinduism. The *Bhagavad Gītā* contains most of the essential teachings of the *Upanishads*, giving it a status very close to that of the *Upanishads*.

THE TANTRAS

Side by side with the Vedic disciplines, Hinduism has another parallel set of disciplines called the Tantras.[7] In the disciplines of Tantra, God is looked upon as both a Male and a Female principle, called *Shiva* and *Shakti* respectively.

Shakti is the creative power of Shiva. In modern scientific terms, Shiva can be compared to potential energy and Shakti to kinetic energy. When potential energy becomes active it is called kinetic energy. When Shiva becomes active, He is called Shakti. Conversely, when Shakti is inactive, She is called Shiva. It is Shakti which

---

7. In Sanskrit: *Tanyate vistāryate jnānam anena iti tantram*—"the scripture by which knowledge is spread is called Tantra."

has created this world. The relationship between Shiva and Shakti is like the relationship between fire and its burning power. They are always inseparable and one. Shakti, however, has many other names. One of them is Pārvatī.

The scriptural texts of Tantra are usually in the form of dialogues between Shiva and Pārvatī. The dialogues where Shiva is the speaker giving spiritual teachings and Pārvatī is the listener are called *Āgama* texts. Where Pārvatī plays the role of teacher and Shiva the listener, the texts are called *Nigama*.

Tantra is an all-inclusive religious system which is capable of helping man at all levels of spiritual growth. It has spiritual disciplines suitable for people from the highest cultural level to the lowest.

 The Tantra literature is vast. Among the 64 most prominent texts, we can mention *Mahānirvāna, Kulasāra, Prapanchasāra, Kulārnava, Rudra Yāmala, Vishnu Yāmala, Brahma Yāmala* and *Tantrarāja*.

SHAIVA ĀGAMAS AND PANCHARĀTRA SAMHITĀS

Shaiva Āgamas are related to the Tantras. Of the original 28 *Shaiva Āgamas* only 20 are available now.

Pancharātra Samhitās are the scriptures of certain Vaishnava sects of Hinduism. The number of scriptural texts pertaining to these Samhitās is 250; of them *Brihad-Brahma, Īshvara* and *Jnānāmritasāra Samhitās* are particularly noteworthy.

IV

INDO-ARYANS & THEIR SOCIETY

THEORIES CONCERNING THE ORIGIN OF THE INDO-ARYANS

It is very difficult to arrive at any definite decision about the original home of the Indo-Aryans. There is considerable controversy among scholars about where they came from. For many decades archaeologists, anthropologists, historians and philologists have independently or conjointedly been trying to discover the original home of the Indo-Aryans. Through their research they have developed various theories, but have not yet been able to arrive at a common conclusion.

It is generally believed that the ancestors of the Indo-Aryans were not indigenous to India, but migrated from some other region. According to some scholars, such as Gafurov,[1] they came from Central Asia. According to Tilak, the forefathers of the Indo-Aryans came from the Arctic.[2] Bender thought that the ancestors of the Indo-Aryans most probably came from the region where the Lithuanians have lived "for at least five thousand years." Bongard-Levin is of the opinion that the ancestral home

1. Bobodzhan Gafurovich Gafurov, *From Ancient History to Contempory Times* (Delhi, India: Navayug Publishers, 1973), 141 & 149.
2. Lokamanya Bal Gangadhar Tilak, *The Arctic Home in The Vedas* (Puna City, India: Tilak Bros., 1956), 388-389.

of the Aryans was the region of southeastern Europe between the Dnieper and the Ural mountains.[3,4] Some say that the migration of the Indo-Aryans into India probably started around 1700 B.C. and continued till 1200 B.C.[5] However, Swāmī Vivekānanda, one of the greatest exponents of Hinduism, believed that the Indo-Aryans were indigenous to India, and had not come from anywhere else.[6]

ARYANS AND THEIR GOTRA

In ancient times the Aryans were nomadic people. They had not yet formed an urban society. Their wealth and livelihood depended mainly on raising cattle. They constantly herded their cattle from one grazing ground to another. In certain seasons the cattle needed protection from the ravages of harsh weather. During a severe winter or the rainy season the cattle were kept in secure shelters.

A shelter for cattle is called a *gotra* in Sanskrit. As these shelters were relatively small in number, many Indo-Aryan families were obliged to put their cattle in the same shelter or gotra. As a result, the cattle of one family often got mixed up with the cattle of other families and disputes arose over their ownership. To resolve such disputes, supervisors were appointed to act as judges and give fair and just verdicts.

---

3. Harold H. Bender, *The Home of the Indo-Europeans* (Princeton: Princeton University Press, 1922), 55.
4. G. M. Bongard-Levin, *The Origin of the Aryans* (Delhi, India: Arnold-Heinemann, 1980), 123.
5. C. P. Masica, *The Indo-Aryan Languages* (New York: Cambridge University Press, 1991), 37.
6. *The Complete Works of Swāmī Vivekānanda*, vol. 3 (Calcutta: Advaita Ashrama), 293.

These supervisors were endowed with great moral and spiritual virtues. They were appointed as supervisors because of their exalted character and were called *Gotrapati*, meaning Lord or Master of the Gotra. Some of them were later recognized as spiritually illumined souls. Among these highly venerated Gotrapatis are Shāndilya, Bharadvāja, Kāshyapa and others, who are considered to be *rishis* (*lit.*, seer or overseer) or sages.

When an Aryan of one clan or family met someone belonging to another Aryan clan or family, he introduced himself by using the name of his Gotrapati, such as Shāndilya or Bharadvāja. The descendants of these Aryans, now called Hindus, carry on that same tradition and use the Gotrapati's name to identify themselves. Every Hindu, therefore, is expected to remember the name of his ancestral Gotra. To avoid inbreeding, marriage between members of the same Gotra was forbidden. But, now that many centuries have passed, that custom is not followed as strictly.

THE CASTE SYSTEM

Originally the caste system had a qualitative basis and all castes were treated equally

Indo-Aryans were divided into four castes or social categories, known as the Caste System. Such division was originally based on the inherent qualities or "career potential" of the individuals. A person naturally endowed with noble qualities like truthfulness, serenity of mind, nonviolence, compassion, and unselfishness belonged to the *Brahmin* or priestly caste. Possessed of great spiritual and moral virtues, he was considered the right person to teach and give spiritual guidance to others. One naturally endowed with martial qualities was fit for the *Kshatriya* or military caste. Kings and administrators generally came from the Kshatriya caste. Similarly, anyone naturally gifted with business acumen belonged to the *Vaishya* or merchant caste. Others belonged to the *Shūdra* caste.[7] This fourth caste included laborers and artisans, etc.

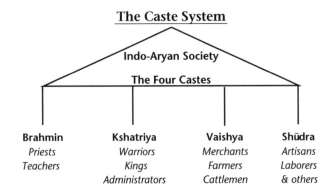

The Caste System

Indo-Aryan Society

The Four Castes

Brahmin	**Kshatriya**	**Vaishya**	**Shūdra**
Priests	*Warriors*	*Merchants*	*Artisans*
Teachers	*Kings*	*Farmers*	*Laborers*
	Administrators	*Cattlemen*	*& others*

Aryans who were exempted from the caste system, and the outcastes or untouchables

Not all Aryans adhered to the caste system. For instance, all-renouncing monks or *Sannyāsins* were beyond caste rules. Though not belonging to any caste, they were respected by one and all. Non-Aryans, and the progeny of Aryans who violated the laws of Aryan society pertaining to food, matrimony, and so on, were usually considered outcastes. According to Manu, the most

---

7. Some historians think that the Shūdras were originally of non-Aryan origin, but were later adopted by the Aryan society. See R.C. Majumdar & H.C. Raychaudhuri, *An Advanced History of India* (London: MacMillan & Co., 1948), 32.

famous lawgiver, "A twice-born man who knowingly eats mushrooms, a village pig, garlic, a village cock, onions, or leeks, will become an outcaste."[8,9]

Outcastes, for obvious reasons, did not enjoy the same status as those belonging to the caste system. They had lower status in Aryan society, but there is no evidence to prove that they were ill-treated or hated at that time. Much later, during the decadent stage of the caste system, outcastes were treated as inferior and given the name "untouchables."

Caste system became degraded when made hereditary

Originally every caste was given equal importance. Each was considered essential for Aryan society. Later, as time passed, vested interests crept in. Caste, originally determined by the qualities and aptitudes of the individual, was made hereditary by self-interested people in positions of power and authority. They wanted to perpetuate their caste-based social privileges. As a result, the caste system degenerated. Some castes were artificially made superior or "higher" and others inferior or "lower."

Brahmins, who belonged to the highest caste, comprised the learned priestly class. Traditionally they were not rich. Nevertheless, they held positions of respect and honor in society. Kshatriyas, belonging to the second highest caste, held the positions of kings, administrators, or warriors and could enjoy wealth and power. Vaishyas belonged to the next lower caste. Even though they could never be priests, kings or military officers, they could find

8. Twice-born means belonging to any but the Shūdra caste.
9. F. Max Müller, *Laws of Manu* (Delhi, India: Motilal Banarasidas, 1979), V/19.

satisfaction from wealth earned through trade. But Shūdras, reduced to the lowest caste and denied many privileges, including Vedic and other higher education, suffered the most. This disparity in privileges corrupted the caste system and eventually bred intercaste jealousy, hatred, and conflict. Under these circumstances, the condition of the untouchables or the outcastes became even worse.

The effects of repeated foreign aggression on Hindu India and the caste system

As centuries passed, Aryan society underwent a lot of change. Starting in 327 B.C., India was repeatedly invaded by many foreign aggressors, including the Greeks, Huns, Arabs, Turks, Afghans, Persians, Mongols, Portuguese, French and British. From the 13th century onwards the Muslims ruled the greater part of India for nearly 600 years, until the British took over power at the end of the 18th century. India shook off the British rule in 1947 and became an independant nation. All these invasions, many years of foreign rule, and the passage of time left their impact on Hindu society. As a result, society changed, and the caste system changed along with it.

During the British rule, the Brahmins were the first to benefit from English education. Giving up their caste-based traditional professions of priesthood and teaching, many became medical doctors, engineers, businessmen, government servants, and lawyers. Brahmins even went into military service. Members of the other higher castes who took advantage of English education also enjoyed similar opportunities. Still the fate of the culturally and economically disadvantaged members of the lowest caste and the untouchables remained more or less the same.

Even though the original character of the caste system was changed beyond recognition, the false sense of superiority of one caste over another still lingered on in some parts of India.

Steps taken to cure the degraded caste system

Since becoming an independent nation in 1947, the government of India has given all citizens of India, irrespective of caste, color, sex or religion, equal access to higher education and other facilities provided by the government. Special scholarships and stipends are given to members of the underprivileged classes to encourage them to pursue higher education. The government also passed a law in 1949 banning untouchability.

Through the years many Hindu saints have strongly disapproved of the decadent caste system and refused even to recognize it. For instance, both Shrī Chaitanya[10] and Shrī Rāmakrishna[11] taught their followers that lovers of God do not have any caste whatsoever. Many social reformers also condemned the degenerated caste system. Mahātmā Gāndhī (1869–1948), the well-known freedom fighter and political leader of India, was very critical of the ills of this system.

Thinking people of India today unanimously condemn the severely weakened and yet lingering specter of the caste system. Yet some politicians and others with

10. Shrī Chaitanya (1485-1533). Well-known saint; revered by many as a Divine Incarnation. See *An Advanced History of India* editd by R.C. Majumdar, H.C. Raychaudhuri & Kalikinkar Datta. Macmillan & Co. Ltd. 1948.
11. Shrī Rāmakrishna (1836-1886). Well-known saint of modern India; considered by many to be a Divine Incarnation and a prophet of the harmony of all religions.

Mahātmā Gāndhī

ulterior motives try to keep the system alive by promoting intercaste hatred and conflict. Nevertheless, their efforts are bound to fail, because more and more people are getting educated and no longer believe in this system. Eventually, educating the masses and improving their living standard, coupled with a healthy religious education, will eradicate this decadent system. As proof of this, some intercaste marriages have lately been taking place among the educated and relatively more affluent urban population of India.

While India has its caste system, Europe has its "class system," and the United States has its own social strata based on wealth. Swāmī Vivekānanda used to say that any attempt to remove the caste system forcibly will only cause a similar system to take its place. According to him, efforts should be made to

Shrī Chaitanya

raise the educational, cultural and economic levels of Hindus from the so-called lower castes up to the cultural level of the so-called highest caste Brahmins. Pulling the Brahmins down to the level of the culturally disadvantaged lowest caste is not a healthy solution. It will only cause further degradation of the Hindu society.

THE FOUR STAGES OF ARYAN LIFE

In ancient times the Hindus, known then as Aryans, were expected to go through the four stages of Aryan life:

- *Brahmacharya*—the stage of a student
- *Gārhasthya*—the stage of a householder or family man
- *Vānaprasthya*—the stage of a retired person or hermit
- *Sannyāsa*—the stage of a monk or ascetic

Four Stages of Indo-Aryan Life

First	Second	Third	Fourth
Student	Householder	Retired Person or Hermit	Monk or Ascetic

Brahmacharya—the first stage of ancient Aryan life

In order to be educated, every Aryan boy between the ages of seven and eleven had to go and live in his teacher's home, where he remained until his education was finished. Normally it would take about twelve years to complete his education. During that period he was required to practice complete celibacy and imbibe noble virtues, as well as get a formal education. Great emphasis was put on developing character.

The role model for the student was his teacher, who was endowed with many noble, moral and spiritual qualities. The teacher would not only give the students secular education, but he was also their spiritual guide. In addition to the study of the Vedas, the student studied grammar, poetry, ethics, morals, mathematics, and astronomy. Yet the students were emphatically told that the final aim of education was liberation through God-vision.

The teacher looked upon his students as his own children and gave them the same amount of love and affection. The students also considered their teacher's home their own and helped with various household chores. A student was called an *antevāsin*. The teacher was called the *guru* or *āchārya* in Sanskrit. This period of studentship was the first stage of Aryan life.

The relationship between the teacher and the student was not based on money. The teacher would not accept any fee or salary. It was against Aryan tradition to accept remuneration for any kind of teaching—spiritual or secular. The teacher, usually a family man, lived a simple life devoid of luxury. What few wants he had were most often met by occasional gifts from the king. The students were not a financial burden on their teacher. It was customary for the students to go to the neighbors' homes every day and beg for food. They wore deerskin or processed tree-bark, a grass girdle and matted locks. The cows owned by their teacher provided them with plenty of nutritious milk.

On completion of his education the student was called a *snātaka*, which means a "bather." The word implies that the student had successfully bathed in the water of knowledge. In today's language, becoming a snātaka would be like graduating from college. After graduation the students gave gifts to the teacher as a token of their respect and gratitude. There was a farewell meeting, and the teacher gave a final address to the students. The *Taittirīya Upanishad*, a part of the Vedas, has the following farewell address given by a teacher to his departing students.[12] This address will convey some idea about the duties and ideals of the students of the Vedic period:

> Let your conduct be marked by right action, including study and teaching of the scriptures; by truthfulness in word, deed, and thought; by self-denial and the practice of austerity; by poise and self-control; by performance of the everyday duties of life with a cheerful heart and an unattached mind.

> Speak the truth. Do your duty. Do not neglect the study of the scriptures. Do not cut the thread of progeny. Swerve not from truth. Deviate not from the path of the good. Revere greatness.

> Let your mother be a god to you; let your father be a god to you; let your teacher be a god to you; let your guest also be a god to you. Do only such actions as are blameless. Always show reverence to the great.

> Whatever you give to others, give with love and reverence. Gifts must be given in abundance, with joy, humility, and compassion.

---

12. Swāmī Prabhavānanda and Frederick Manchester, *The Upanishads—Breath of the Eternal* (Hollywood, CA: Vedanta Press, 1947), 81-82.

If at any time there is doubt with regard to right conduct, follow the practice of great souls, who are guileless, of good judgment, and devoted to truth.

Thus conduct yourself always. This is the injunction, this is the teaching, and this is the command of the scriptures.

After graduation the students returned home, married and entered the second stage of Aryan life—the stage of a family man or householder.

In ancient times, girls also resided in their teachers' homes and received education similar to that of boys. Later, as society became more rigid, it became customary for girls to be educated at home. They were then taught by their male relatives. The custom of begging food was observed by them only within the confines of their homes. The wearing of deerskin, tree-bark and matted locks by girls was banned. Nevertheless, around the 5th century B.C., there were many learned women teachers enjoying the same status and positions of honor as men teachers did. Among the great women scholars of the Vedic period were Gārgī, the daughter of Vāchaknu, and Pathyasvatī, who for her scholarship was given the title *Vāch*, meaning "the goddess of learning." In the early Vedic period there were also women sages; Vishvavārā, Ghoshā, and Apālā, to name a few. Girls of the Vedic period also learned singing, dancing, the playing of musical instruments, painting, sewing, poetry-writing, carpentry, the making of garlands, and other fine arts.

Nowadays that tradition is no longer followed. Students no longer live and are educated in their teacher's home, nor do they dress in deerskin, bark and grass girdles, or have matted locks. Begging food from neighbors' homes is no longer done. The educational system in India today is exactly like the educational system of any other country in the West. Teachers in schools and colleges work for a salary as their counterparts in western countries do. Teachers give secular education to the students, and society no longer objects to their accepting a salary.

Nevertheless, the ancient tradition of not accepting money for spiritual education is still honored in India. Any spiritual teacher or holy man who violates this rule brings only disgrace to this time-honored tradition of Hinduism.

Whatever changes have occurred in the ancient educational system are mostly the result of nearly two hundred years of British rule in India, which ended in 1947. Now Hindu girls attend western style schools and colleges, some of which are coeducational. Just as the boys do, they study humanities, science, engineering, medicine and arts and crafts. Generally neither boys nor girls study the Vedas anymore. That tradition has gone out of style. Still, they go to temples and observe the rituals of their religion during the many religious festivals celebrated throughout the year.

Gārhasthya—the second stage of ancient Aryan life

This stage of life started with marriage. Upon returning home the student, with the permission of his teacher, married a young woman of his own caste, but not of the same Gotra. After marriage he lived the life of a householder following the dictates of the scriptures.

Among other things, he had to perform the daily worship ritual called the *agnihotra* where fire is used as the symbol of God, study the Vedas regularly, earn an honest living, practice hospitality, raise children, be charitable to the poor, honor his elders, and take care of his parents and the other relatives living with him. According to the sage Manu, the renowned law-giver of ancient India, it was the householder's duty to treat women with honor and respect and make them happy by giving desirable gifts on holidays and festivals. In the words of Manu, "Where the female relations live in grief, the family soon wholly perishes; but that family where they are not unhappy ever prospers."[13]

The husband and wife were expected to observe complete fidelity, and it was their duty to create a happy atmosphere at home. "In that family, where the husband is pleased with his wife and the wife with her husband, happiness will assuredly be lasting," says Manu. Moreover, such a family provided an ideal loving environment for children to grow up in. Great importance was given to raising noble children.

The wife was called *ardhāngini* (lit. having half a body) in the sense that she and her husband were two halves constituting the body of an ideal marriage. She was also called *sahadharminī*, which means "the partner in spiritual life." Both the husband and the wife were expected to help each other in their spiritual growth. A member of Aryan society, no matter in which stage of life, was always reminded that the ultimate goal of human life is God-realization.

13. F. Max Müller, *Sacred Books of The East*, Vol. XXV (New Delhi, India: Motilal Banarsidas, 1979), III/57.

Men were allowed to practice polygamy. A widower could remarry, but usually not a widow who had to practise celibacy and live like a nun.[14] This double standard probably existed because Aryan society at that time was dominated by men. Divorce was not permitted. Marriage was considered a sacrament and was meant to last the entire lifetime of the partners.

In today's Hinduism, however, divorce is permitted by a law enacted in 1955. Another law permitting the remarriage of widows was passed during British rule mainly through the efforts of the great 19th century Hindu reformer and scholar, Īshvar Chandra Vidyāsāgar (1820–1891).[15] In spite of these laws benefiting Hindu women, very few divorces or widow-marriages take place in India except in the lower cultural and economic strata of the country. A negligible number of such cases has also occurred among the wealthy and upper middle-class Hindus in big cities, but they are the exception and not the rule. Despite the legalization of divorce and widow-marriage, some stigma associated with them still persists. Such reforms have not yet been fully approved or accepted by the vast majority of Hindus. The government of India also passed a law banning polygamy; the Muslim population is, however, exempt from this law.[16]

Vānaprasthya—the third stage of ancient Aryan life

According to the law-giver Manu, when a householder

---

14. Remarriage of virgin widows was permitted in the early Vedic period, but later on it was prohibited.

15. Jadunāth Sarkār, *India Through the Ages* (Calcutta, India: M. C. Sarkar & Sons. 1928), 113.

16. To know more about Hindu marriage please see *Hindu Marriage—Ancient and Modern* on page 40.

would "see his skin wrinkled, and his hair white," his time for entering the third stage of life had come. He then retired to the forest, "either committing the care of his wife to his sons, or accompanied by her." He lived in a humble hut, wore bark, animal skin, or tattered clothes; studied the Vedas regularly and performed various worship rituals. His food was mainly vegetables, flowers, fruits and roots, either cooked or uncooked. He had a long beard, didn't cut his hair, nor clip his nails. Or, in other words, he lived a life of great simplicity and religious austerity to achieve the spiritual goal of his life. This stage of life was obviously a preparation for the next stage of Aryan life, the stage of a monk or an ascetic.

As times have changed, Hindus no longer follow this ancient tradition. And yet, with the approach of old age, almost every Hindu starts remembering the ways of his ancestors. Even though not living in the forest, he becomes pensive and starts showing signs of genuine spiritual interest, either in order to depart from this world with dignity, or to have "spiritual liberation." For this purpose many men and women move to holy places of pilgrimage like Vārānasī,[17] and live a retired life of prayer and worship.

Sannyāsa—the fourth stage of ancient Aryan life

This stage of Aryan life was a natural transition from the life of a hermit to the life of an ascetic or a monk. According to Baudhāyana, a law-giver of ancient India, any of the following was fit to enter this stage of life: (1) a

---

17. Vārānasī, formerly known as Benares, is one of the many holy cities of India. It is an ancient city on the bank of the holy river Gangā in the state of Uttar Pradesh.

student who had just completed his period of studentship and was feeling an inner urge to renounce the
world, (2) a childless householder, (3) a widower, (4) a
wanderer and (5) a hermit. Anyone who was seventy
years old and whose children had become settled in life
was also considered fit to renounce the world and
become a monk.

An ascetic or monk regularly shaved his head, clipped
his nails, and sustained his body by begging food every
day from a maximum of seven homes. He slept under a
tree, in a temple, or in an abandoned house. He constantly wandered from one place to another carrying a
staff, begging bowl and water pot, no longer wearing the
white clothes of the householder. He would not stay in
any one place for more than a few days. He was
exempted from performing the agnihotra and other
obligatory rituals required of the Aryans belonging to
other stages of life. Nevertheless, he had to study the
Vedas regularly.

According to the monastic ideal, a monk belongs to the
entire world. Consequently, he severed all ties with his
family. He took the vows of nonviolence, truthfulness,
non-stealing, abstinence and tolerance. He obeyed his
spiritual teacher, abstained from anger, avoided rashness
of thought or action, and followed rules of cleanliness
and purity about eating. He was required to think of himself as essentially the effulgent soul or Ātman, and not an
embodied being. His goal was to become a God-realized
soul by realizing his identity with Brahman (God).

The Hindu monks of today more or less follow that
same ancient ideal of *Sannyāsa* or monasticism. Orga-
nized monasticism, however, was first introduced to the

world by Gautama Buddha nearly 2500 years ago and later adopted by Hinduism.

Shankara, the great 8th century Hindu saint and philosopher of India, founded a monastic order known as the *Dashnāmī* Order. This order is not as well-organized and regimented as the Buddhist monastic order, but through the centuries it has played a very important role in Hinduism. Following the old and orthodox Hindu tradition, it mainly stresses individual spiritual growth along with the study and teaching of the scriptures.

The Rāmakrishna Mission, a well-known monastic order founded on modern lines by Swāmī Vivekānanda at the turn of the 20th century, encourages its members to engage in various philanthropic and humanitarian activities side-by-side with scriptural studies and spiritual practice. Their ideal is to serve man as God and also to strive for their own spiritual enlightenment. The Rāmakrishna Mission is the largest and most well-organized Hindu monastic order in India today. This monastic order, although an independent organization, owes its lineage to Shankara. Its monks, by tradition, belong to the *Purī* branch of the Dashnāmī Order.

Today's Hinduism, like any other ancient religion, has many denominations or sects. Many of these sects have their own brands of monasticism based on the ancient Vedic ideal of asceticism.

V

HINDUISM—A WAY OF LIFE

Many scholars have rightly described Hinduism as a way of life. Every important event of Hindu life has to be sanctified through religious observance. This ritualistic sanctification or sacrament is called *samskāra* in Sanskrit. There are ten such samskāras, pertaining to (1) marriage, (2) the consummation of marriage, (3) prayers for the well-being of a pregnant woman, (4) the birth of a child, (5) naming of the baby, (6) giving the baby its first solid food, (7) the baby's first hair-cut, (8) introduction of the child to his studies, (9) *Upanayana* or the sacred thread ceremony,[1] and (10) the returning home ceremony after a student completes his education at the teacher's home.[2] For every such event specific worship ritual has to be performed.

---

1. In the Vedic period boys of the three higher castes, before attaining puberty, had to go through a spiritual initiation called the *Upanayana* ceremony. During that ceremony they would be invested with a sanctified or sacred girdle to be worn by them all the time, and particularly when performing worship rituals. This girdle, also called the *upavīta*, would be made of grass, fibers or threads.
2. In the Vedic period students had to live in their teacher's home for several years until their graduation. Upon their return home a special religious ritual would be observed. This tradition is no longer followed today. The system of education in India has changed and is now very similar to that in the West.

Other than the above, there are prescribed religious rituals for (1) the funeral for the departed, (2) the post-funeral honoring of the departed (*Shrāddha Ceremony*), (3) building a new home, (4) entering a new home, (5) spiritual initiation, and (6) the attainment of puberty for girls.

Today, because of the changed times and altered lifestyles of the Hindus, not all the samskāras mentioned above are strictly followed. Under special circumstances such lapses are condoned by Hinduism. For instance, the scriptures say that a Hindu need not strictly observe the scriptural injunctions and prohibitions in a foreign land if the circumstances there are not conducive to such an observance.

HINDU MARRIAGES—ANCIENT & MODERN

Hindu society is much more family-oriented and close-knit than societies in the West. The average size of a typical Hindu family is generally much larger than a family in the West. Married sons live with their parents, brothers, unmarried sisters, and also grandparents. Young women, when married, go to the homes of their in-laws to live with their husbands. There are very few nuclear families in Hindu society.

Maintaining the good image of the family is considered one of the primary duties of the family members. The respectability of a Hindu family is determined by the moral virtues of its members and its cultural level, and not necessarily by its wealth. Every member of a family is expected to uphold or enhance the good image of the family by maintaining its moral and cultural level.

An important event like the marriage of a family member is bound to have its impact on the entire family. None should enter into a matrimonial relationship which will adversely affect the image of the family. A Hindu marriage is not just a relationship between a husband and wife; it also engenders a close and lasting relationship between the members of both families. It is sometimes said, and not too incorrectly, that a Hindu marriage is more a marriage between two families than between two persons.

In general, Hindu marriages are arranged by the parents or guardians of the young people. In the rare cases where young men or women choose their own marriage partners, the approval of the parents or the guardians must be obtained. Otherwise it may cause a lot of heartache or sadness for both the families involved. Parents, being more experienced, are usually able to select a good marriage partner for their son or daughter. They make thorough inquiries about not only their future daughter-in-law or son-in-law, but their families as well. During the negotiations, the intended couple are allowed to see each other only once or twice in the presence of family members. If they like each other and give their consent, then their marriage is arranged by the parents or guardians. No premarital dating or free mixing between men and women, as in the West, is allowed in Hindu society. According to available statistics, such arranged marriages are many times more harmonious and stable than marriages where the partners choose each other.[3]

---

3. To know more about arranged marriages please read Mrs. Majumdar's views on page 56.

In ancient times the following eight types of marriage took place in Aryan society:

- In *Brāhma Marriage* the father or guardian gave away his daughter "decked with costly garments and jewels" to a carefully chosen bridegroom well-versed in the Vedas and endowed with noble qualities. The bride's father also honored the bridegroom by offering him a traditional drink made of honey.
- In *Daiva Marriage* the daughter, "duly decked with ornaments," was given in gratitude to a priest for performing some important worship ritual. Such a marriage, however, was rare.
- In *Ārsha Marriage* the bride's father received a gift of a milk cow and a breeding bull from the bridegroom. This gift, permitted by the sacred lawbooks, was a token of respect—not a dowry.[4]
- In *Prājāpatya Marriage* the bride's father gave his daughter away to the bridegroom with this traditional blessing: "May both of you perform your duties together." The bridegroom was also honored by being given a traditional honeyed drink.
- In *Gāndharva Marriage* the bridegroom and bride married secretly without the knowledge of their parents or guardians.
- In *Āsura Marriage* the bridegroom voluntarily gave as much wealth as he could afford to the bride and her relatives,[5] and then received the bride as his wife.

---

4. In ancient times dairy cattle were the main wealth of the Hindus, hence such a gift.
5. Such gifts were not in accordance with the injunctions of the sacred law. The lawgiver Manu did not approve of this because it was like buying the bride by paying money.

- In *Rākshasa Marriage* the girl was forcibly taken away from her family and then persuaded to marry.
- In *Paishācha Marriage* a person married a girl whom he had seduced while she was asleep, intoxicated or insane.

Among all these marriages, brāhma marriage was considered superior to the others. The lawgiver Manu prohibited āsura and paishācha marriages. Gāndharva and rākshasa marriages were also considered inferior because they were caused by lustful impulses. Only the kshatriyas were permitted to have gāndharva and rākshasa marriages. During the time of Manu the kshatriyas, who were either rulers or warriors, considered rākshasa marriage an act of bravery. To capture a woman the kshatriyas had to fight with her relatives. They had to risk their lives to wed a woman of their own choice. It also appears that the kshatriyas, more than others, indulged in gāndharva marriages. Aside from that, it was the duty of the kings to enforce the laws governing society. Manu obviously chose the path of least resistance. He did not want to antagonize the kings who were kshatriyas.

Brāhma marriage is observed by Hindus today. Either giving or taking a dowry in marriage is strongly condemned by various sages and scriptures of Hinduism. For instance, ancient law books such as the *Āpastamba Smriti* and *Manu Smriti*; scriptures such as the *Nārada Purāna*; and sages like Sanatkumāra, have strongly condemned the dowry system. Nevertheless, in certain parts of India today, the bride's parents are often pressured by the bridegroom's family to give a dowry for their daughter's marriage. This practice, in violation of the dictates of the scriptures and the saints, has turned into a social evil. Should other efforts fail, young and idealistic Hindu men and women must come forward and start a movement to eradicate this evil.

A Hindu marriage consists of five important ceremonies:

- *Vāgdāna*—the verbal contract between the fathers or guardians about the marriage of the young man and woman
- *Kanyā Sampradāna*—giving away the daughter to the bridegroom by her father or guardian
- *Varana*—welcoming the bride and the bridegroom
- *Pāṇigrahana*—ritualistic holding of each other's hands by the bride and the bridegroom
- *Saptapadī*—the seven step walking ritual by the bride and the bridegroom

The entire marriage procedure for the bride and bridegroom is an elaborate religious ritual consisting of fasting, prayer, worship, and some festivities. The exchange of rings and garlands is also a part of Hindu marriage ritual. The marriage ritual starts with the Vāgdāna ceremony and ends with the Saptapadī ceremony. The marriage generally takes place in the bride's home. After the marriage the bride goes with the groom to her in-laws' home where other religious rituals connected with their marriage take place. There is no honeymoon in a Hindu marriage. During these ceremonies many friends and relatives are invited and treated with sumptuous feasts in both the homes. The bride is usually lavished with various gifts by the invited guests and relatives.

Different dictates have been given by the ancient scriptures and law books of Hinduism regarding the marriageable age of the bride and bridegroom. According to one such dictate, the bridegroom should be twice the age of the bride. According to another, the bridegroom should be twenty-five and the bride sixteen. Marriage of a young man under twenty-one was not recommended by the scriptures. These ancient rules are not strictly followed by today's Hindus.

Today a typical Hindu young man living in a city is likely to marry between the ages of 25 and 30. He may not think of marriage until he has a comfortable income. He is expected to marry a woman of his own caste but not his own Gotra.[6] He is likely to marry a woman younger than he. Preferably she should be of a financial, cultural and educational background similar to his own.

In rural areas, however, children of farmers and land owners marry relatively younger. Three or four generations ago many boys and girls in villages married before attaining puberty. Such child marriages were later consummated through a religious ceremony when both the girls and boys became adults. These child marriages, however, have been legally banned in India for many years.[7]

Although the main rituals of Hindu marriage are generally observed everywhere, secondary rituals connected with marriage may differ from place to place. Such

---

6. For the meaning of the word *gotra* please see page 22.
7. In 1929, the Sārdā Act was passed banning the marriage of girls under fourteen. In 1955, the Hindu Marriage Act was passed, raising the minimum age of marriage to 15 for girls and 18 for boys.

variation is due to different local customs or family traditions. Hindus of certain smaller sects and those who belong to the lower cultural and economic strata of Hindu society follow relatively simplified versions of Hindu marriage.

Priests are usually appointed to conduct traditional Hindu marriages. Marriages officiated by priests are considered sacraments; they are not required by Hindu law to be registered. However, in some cities a small number of registered marriages, conducted by judges or registrars of marriages, have lately been taking place. These marriages are usually intercaste marriages,[8] or marriages which would not be easily approved of or condoned by Hindu society.

During the Vedic period, there was some provision for the remarriage of virgin widows, but no provision for divorce. Hindu marriage is a lifelong commitment—a sacrament never to be broken through separation. Its foundation is chastity, fidelity and mutual trust between the husband and wife. Nevertheless, through the Hindu Marriage Act of 1955, divorce was legalized by the Indian Parliament. To this day, however, there are very few divorces in Hindu society. The vast majority of Hindus have not yet wholeheartedly approved of this reform. Indulging in divorce is still bound to tarnish the image of any respectable Hindu family.

Although permitted by law, Hindu widows with children rarely remarry. A Hindu mother is highly adored

---

8. Act III of 1873 and the later Gour Act provide scope for intercaste marriages. In 1949, the Hindu Marriage Validating Act was passed to remove all barriers to intercaste marriage.

and loved by her children. To them she is the embodiment of chastity and purity. Her remarriage would be a
terrible shock to her children. Hindu legends and history
are full of stories of ideal Hindu women who would
rather kill themselves by taking poison or jumping into
fire than lose their bodily purity and chastity. When a
woman becomes a widow, either her husband's family or
her own family comes forward to take care of her and her
children. She does not feel helpless or abandoned by her
relatives.

HINDU FUNERALS

Hindus generally cremate their dead. The body of the
departed is given a bath and dressed in fresh clothes. Fra-
grant sandalwood paste is applied to the corpse, which is
then decorated with flowers and garlands, followed by a
small amount of gold dust sprinkled on different parts of
the head and face. After some purificatory scriptural
chants and worship rituals, the body is placed on the
funeral pyre facing either north or south. A close relative
of the departed, preferably the eldest son, lights some
kindling and walks around the pyre chanting a prayer for
the well-being of the departed soul. Then he lights the
funeral pyre after touching the mouth of the departed
with kindling. In some big cities of India, bodies are cremated in modern crematoria. The same is true for Hindus
living in the West. The ashes are later put in a holy river
or in the sea. As all holy rivers eventually pour into the
sea, the sea is considered very holy.

The body of a Hindu saint is not usually cremated. It is
either put in a grave or buried in water. In a water-burial
the body is securely tied to a long and flat piece of heavy

VI

HINDU SOCIETY TODAY

FAMILY STRUCTURE

Today's Hindu society is very different from the society of the Vedic period. Nevertheless, some of the old traditions are still being followed partially or in modified forms. Hindus do not go through the four stages of life anymore, as their Vedic ancestors did. After student life, barring a few exceptions, a Hindu enters the stage of a family man and remains there until death. He does not go through the stages of a hermit or an ascetic anymore.

Nearly ninety per cent of the people of India live in villages. The people of rural India depend mainly on farming for their livelihood. Even two generations ago most Hindus lived in large joint or extended families. Married sons would live with their parents, brothers, unmarried sisters, uncles, aunts, cousins, nephews, nieces, and grandparents. The produce of the farm would usually maintain such large families. Today, due to economic reasons and population explosion, the joint family system has been breaking up, giving rise to smaller families—though the tradition of married sons living with their parents and unmarried brothers and sisters is still followed by Hindus.

As rural farms in most cases are no longer able to support the ever-increasing number of families, some smaller families have been moving to the cities to make a living. As a result, some nuclear families are gradually forming in the urban societies, but their number is still small.

A superficial observation of a Hindu family may give the impression that it is a male-dominated one. The father, who is usually the principal breadwinner, appears to be the most authoritative figure. Children hold him in awe because he is the disciplinarian of the family.

Yet it is the mother who really rules the family through her love, kindness, and subtle persuasions. To a Hindu son, the mother's position is the highest; she is the very emblem of purity. He will never tolerate any indignity shown to his mother by anyone; nor will he tolerate any insult done to his father.

Every member of Hindu society is trained to uphold the respectable image of his or her family. Hindu boys and girls are taught to maintain the purity of their bodies until they are married. Free mixing between young men and women is not allowed. There is no dating in Hindu society.

The relationship between brothers and sisters is very close in this society. Both the brother and the sister gladly make great sacrifices for each other, whenever needed. If the mother dies, the elder sister becomes like a mother to her younger brothers and sisters. Similarly, when his father dies, the eldest son takes care of his mother and his younger brothers and sisters. There have been numerous cases where the eldest son, after his father's premature death, has taken care of the entire family for years, spending all his income for them without thinking of his own interest or comfort. Such men are highly adored by Hindu society.

It is not to be supposed, however, that there is no selfishness in Hindu society. Selfishness is universal. It exists in Hindu society as well. However, the Hindu value system strongly condemns it. For instance, a son with a comfortable income who does not take care of his elderly or financially handicapped parents is considered by society to be no better than an animal. In Hindu society money does not necessarily bring respectability. What generates respectability is a person's noble qualities and cultural and educational level.

TREATMENT OF CHILDREN IN HINDU SOCIETY

Children who grow up in a typical Hindu family with their grandparents, uncles or aunts have a special advantage. They are never wanting in genuine love and attention. Such children are lucky not to be at the mercy of questionable babysitters, who work for a fee. They develop healthier minds as a result of growing up in an environment of love and affection. In addition, they learn many valuable traditions from their grandparents. In a larger family, a child learns to adjust to the other members. He learns to share and make sacrifices for others. This training helps the child immensely, not only in his childhood, but also when he grows up. In some urban nuclear families of India, where both the parents have to work owing to economic or other reasons, the children are deprived of these advantages.

Hindu society respects its elderly members. Hindu children are taught to be obedient and respectful to their elders. Talking back disrespectfully to one's parents or elders is considered uncivilized behavior. Such behavior brings disgrace to the entire family.

Through the religious legends and epics of Hinduism, children are made acquainted with role models of morality, ethics and spirituality—such as Rāma, Prahlāda, Nachiketā, Sītā, Sāvitrī, Dhruva, and many others. Moreover, social pressure on individuals to uphold good standards of morality and ethics also persuades Hindu parents to behave in a manner which is inspiring to their children. Unless the parents are good and noble, it is a futile dream to expect the children to grow up into good and noble members of any society.

It may finally be noted that because they are always surrounded by a large number of loving relatives, abuse of children cannot easily take place. Children are punished if they misbehave, but not abused.

CONDITION OF WOMEN IN TODAY'S HINDU SOCIETY

Motherhood is considered the greatest glory of Hindu women. The *Taittirīya Upanishad* teaches, "Mātridevo bhava"—"Let your mother be a god to you." Hindu tradition recognizes mother and motherland as even superior to heaven. The epic *Mahābhārata* says, "While a father is superior to ten Brahmin priests well-versed in the Vedas, a mother is superior to ten such fathers, or the entire world." In Hinduism, God is also looked upon as the Divine Mother. Blessings of both the mother and father are sought by the children in order to succeed in life. Motherly love is considered the most unselfish love. When a mother takes care of her baby, all that she wants is the well-being of the baby. She does not want anything in return. This makes her love superior to other forms of worldly love. These are the reasons why a Hindu mother is highly adored by her children. To her children, she is the very embodiment of chastity, purity and selfless love. Hindu society will never tolerate any insult done to a mother or sister. A riot may start in India to punish the miscreant if the chastity of a Hindu mother or girl is known to have been forcibly violated. To understand the position of women in Hindu society, one has to recognize these Hindu sentiments.

In ancient India, Hindu women did not veil their faces and they enjoyed a considerable amount of freedom in society. But repeated attacks on Hindu India by foreigners through the centuries changed that situation. During such aggressions, and also when India was under foreign occupation, the honor and chastity of women often became the casualties. There have been numerous cases when Hindu women killed themselves rather than yield to indignities inflicted by the aggressors. As a result, Hindu society became more and more protective about its women. The freedom of women was curtailed. To protect themselves Hindu women started covering their faces with veils. They were no longer allowed to have their formal education away from home. Instead, they stayed at home, had whatever education was available there, or none at all. Their participation in social events was greatly restricted.

In the latter half of the 19th century, during the British rule, a few reform movements were started in India to remedy some of the ills of Hindu society, and to prevent the conversion of Hindus to other religions. A great reformer, Rājā Rāmmohan Roy (1772–1833) believed,

Rājā Rāmmohan Roy

among other things, in giving higher education and more social freedom to women. He founded a religious organization called the Brāhmo Samāj, which started many schools for women in India. Swāmī Dayānanda Sarasvatī (1824–1883), the founder of the Ārya Samāj, also believed in the education of women. According to Swāmī Vivekānanda, the founder of the Rāmakrishna Mission, "There is no chance for the welfare of the world unless the condition of women is improved. It is not possible for a bird to fly on one wing only." The Rāmakrishna Mission runs many model educational institutions for both men and women in India.

Those reform movements and the political freedom which India gained in the year 1947 have helped improve the condition of Hindu women immensely. Today's Hindu women enjoy considerable freedom in society. They have the same opportunities which men enjoy in education and other areas of human achievement. Now there are numerous women medical doctors, nurses, engineers, university professors, scientists, philosophers, lawyers, judges, politicians, administrators, social workers, artists, actresses, musicians and dancers in India. For example, Indirā Gāndhī, a Hindu woman, was the prime

Swāmī Dayānanda Sarasvatī

minister of India, and other Hindu women hold high positions in the police and defense forces of the government of India. The number of such women has been steadily and rapidly increasing. Hindu women are not lagging behind the men in their pursuit of adventure. Two women have successfully climbed Mount Everest, one of them twice. A Hindu woman has swum across the English channel. There are mountaineering teams consisting of only women, and Hindu women regularly take part in national or international competitions in athletics and other sports.

Even two generations ago almost all Hindu women were financially dependent on their husbands, but not anymore. In many urban as well as rural families, both the husbands and wives earn money. In many families where there are no sons and the parents are elderly and financially inadequate, unmarried working daughters support their parents. India does not yet have social security or similar government welfare plans for the retired or the elderly, which explains why elderly parents have to depend on their grown children, financially or otherwise.

Western media often speak disapprovingly of Indian parents' reluctance to have girl-children. In this connection Mrs. Līlā Majumdar[1] wrote forty years ago, "It is generally supposed that in middle-class Indian families the problem of providing her marriage expenses is so acute as to render a girl-child unwelcome to her own parents. One must understand that lack of affection for the daughter is not the reason for this attitude, but anxiety for her future. Once again, with the growing popularity of education, it must of necessity soon be realized that the educated unmarried daughter may be an asset to the family and not a liability. Indeed, in many advanced families such a woman has often proved to be a source of comfort to her parents in their old age."[2] Today, forty years later, Mrs. Majumdar's expectation has been fulfilled.

Regarding arranged marriages, which are still in vogue in India today, Mrs. Majumdar writes:

"For the foolish and utterly ignorant marriage is indeed a denial of self-expression, but for the wise and the educated it is the noblest career the world has to offer. A good marriage gives such opportu-

---

1. Formerly Professor at Visvabharati University in Santiniketan, and Asutosh College and Vidyasagar College in Calcutta.
2. Līlā Majumdar, *Great Women of India* (Mayavati, India: Advaita Ashrama, 1953), 119.

nities of fulfillment and service as may never be found elsewhere. To this day the normal Indian woman accepts marriage as her natural destiny, not in perpetual tutelage, as has heretofore been often quoted, a tutelage that commenced under her father, continues under her husband and will end under her son, but as a proper partner, not in rivalry with her husband over personal rights, but bound in service with him for the welfare of the family and the nation.

"To the Western judgment this betokens a slave mentality, but Indian women look upon it otherwise. Indeed, it is an anomaly that in continents where women have fought for their freedom and rights through generations, there should be such feverish competition among almost all adult, even adolescent, women in order to secure a husband at any cost. A glance at the advertisement pages of any popular Western magazine strengthens the idea that the sole aim of dressmakers, chemists and cosmetic manufacturers is so to disguise a plain girl as will enable her to catch a man's eye with matrimony as her final goal. The Indian attitude appears more natural, dignified and simpler in every way. To the Indian girl, even now, marriage is neither frustration nor self-satisfaction, but a self-dedication. An Indian woman, to this day, does not marry her husband alone but adopts his whole family and identifies her own happiness with their well-being. She is bound by ties of duty not only to her husband but also to his parents, brothers, sisters and even nieces and nephews. This imposes a discipline over her emotions and desires, no less rigorous than that of any school. To her eyes the Western idea of family life, which

> excludes and resents a widowed mother's, an
> invalid father's or a ruined brother's claims,
> appears mean and selfish in the extreme. The
> modern Indian woman is no slave to her family,
> but the dispenser of its welfare. She will gladly
> cook, sew, nurse and teach not only for her hus-
> band and children but also for those of his rela-
> tions who may need her services. This is not
> frustration, but the true fulfillment of her woman-
> hood." [3]

Professor Majumdar's above words eloquently express
the ideal of Hindu womanhood, although her opinion of
western women and western family life is open to controversy. No culture or society in this world can claim perfection. Perfection on a societal basis will never be
achieved. Nevertheless, all progressive societies crave perfection. Imperfection in a society is measured by its evils.
And every evil in a society is caused by the selfishness of
one or more of its members. Only the willing and loving
self-sacrifice of its members can make a society better.
Hindu society has been trying to achieve this through its
time-honored ideal of self-sacrifice and service.

---

3. Ibid., 116–117.

VII

THE ROLE OF FOOD

Since the early Vedic period great importance has been given to determining which food can be safely eaten by the Indo-Aryans. Not all kinds of food are considered good for the physical and spiritual well-being of people. The ancient law giver Manu has described in great detail what food is forbidden and what is permitted.[1]

DID THE VEDIC ANCESTORS OF THE HINDUS EAT MEAT?

The Vedic ancestors of the Hindus ate, among other things, certain kinds of meat permitted by their law books (*Smriti*). Though meat eating was permitted, Manu encouraged vegetarianism on grounds of nonviolence. Says Manu, "There is no sin in eating meat...but abstention brings great rewards."[2] But all food, including meat, had to be offered to God first.

A question often asked is whether beef was eaten by the Vedic ancestors of Hindus. There are valid reasons to believe that Vedic Aryans ate beef. But milk cows were never slaughtered. A milk cow was called *aghnyā*, which

---

1. G. Bühler, trans., *The Laws of Manu* (The Oxford University Press, 1886) V/5–56.
2. Ibid., V/56.

Columbia County Library
220 E. Main St.
P.O. Box 668
Magnolia. AR 71754-0668

means "what should not be killed." Only bulls, calves and barren cows were killed for meat.[3]

WHY THE HINDUS OF TODAY DO NOT EAT BEEF

The tradition of not eating beef came to Hinduism much later. Some scholars think that the influence of Jainism[4] might have had something to do with it. Besides that, in rural areas where most of the people of India live, almost every Hindu home has at least one milk cow. Indian cows are very gentle by nature. They are like members of the family. Children grow up drinking their milk and treat them the same way pet dogs are treated in western countries. Apart from the religious taboo in regard to eating beef, this is another reason why a Hindu can never think of killing a cow and eating its meat. Other than that, Hindus always try to avoid slaughtering the females of any animal species as far as practicable.

IS THE COW HOLY?

There is also an idea in the West that Hindus do not eat beef because they consider the cow holy. This notion is not correct. Hinduism, like other theistic religions of the world, believes that God is present everywhere. He is equally present in every being and every thing, but not equally manifest everywhere. God is most manifest in a Divine Incarnation or a saint. He is not as manifest in

---

3. Kunhan Raja, *The Cultural Heritage Of India*, vol. 1 (Calcutta, India: Belur Math), 39.
4. Jainism is an ancient religion. It is an offshoot of Hinduism and is much older than Buddhism. It strongly believes in non-injury to all forms of life.

ordinary human beings, and even less manifest in animals, plants and other "lower" forms of life. He is least manifest in non-living objects like rocks or stones. Therefore, God must be present in a cow also. If not, it will contradict the idea of God's omnipresence. God being the holiest of the holy, whatever has the presence of God in it also has to be holy—why not a cow? However, a Hindu will never consider a cow superior to human beings; the manifestation of God in a cow, an animal, is much less pronounced than in human beings.

In ancient Indo-Aryan nomadic culture, cows had a very useful role. Their milk gave the Aryans nourishment. Browned butter, the main source of edible oil for Aryans, was also used for oil lamps. Shoes and other essential leather goods were made from cow's hide; hooves of cows were used to make glue, and dried cowdung cakes were used as fuel. Thus, probably from a utilitarian point of view, Aryans developed a special feeling of fondness for cows. In some western countries similar sentiments about horses are voiced in statements like, "The horse is a *noble* animal." Such statements are not supposed to be interpreted literally. Just as a thoroughbred is admired as a fine and extremely valuable animal, so also ancient Indo-Aryans might have had a feeling of admiration for cows, and nothing beyond that.

THE RIGHT KINDS OF FOOD AS PRESCRIBED BY THE SCRIPTURES

The *Bhagavad Gītā*, the well-known Hindu scripture, teaches that only juicy, soothing, wholesome and agreeable foods should be taken for one's physical and spiritual well-being. Excessively bitter, sour, too salty, too hot, pungent, dry and burning foods should be avoided. One should also avoid foods which are stale, tasteless, rotten and impure.[5]

The scriptures of the Vaishnava and Shaiva sects of Hinduism prescribe strictly vegetarian food for their followers. Those who belong to the Shākta sect are allowed by their scriptures to take meat, fish and even consecrated wine. As a result some Hindus harbor strong and negative feelings—even hatred—towards Hindus of other sects who eat other kinds of food. The saints, however, have never condoned such negative feelings. Swāmī Vivekānanda lamented, "In India religion has entered into the cooking pot." Shrī Rāmakrishna used to say, "If a person who eats pork[6] can incessantly think of God, then he is far superior to a person who eats vegetarian food and yet thinks of sense objects all the time." Meerā Bāi, the well-known 16th century woman saint of India, used to say:

> Had it been possible for one to see God
> by eating fruits and roots,
> why haven't the bats and monkeys seen Him?
> Had it been possible for one to know God
> by taking baths in the holy waters,
> why haven't the fish known Him?
> Had it been possible for one to find God
> by eating vegetables and leaves,
> why haven't the deer and goats found Him?
> Had it been possible for men to see God
> by renouncing their wives,

---

5. *Bhagavad Gītā*, Chapter XVII, verses 8, 9 and 10.
6. Pork obtained from domesticated pigs is forbidden food according to Hindu tradition.

why haven't the eunuchs seen Him?
Without the love of God, says Meerā,
None can ever have God-vision.[7]

Therefore, according to Hindu saints, eating the right
kind of food, though beneficial for spiritual life, is of secondary importance to developing genuine love of God.
Such love can make God-vision possible.

Meerā Bāi

---

7. Translated by the author.

VIII

GOD

INTRODUCTION

From its beginning, Hinduism has been undergoing evolution. At a very early stage of their civilization the ancestors of the Hindus are believed to have been polytheistic. Earth, water, fire, wind, sky, sun, dawn, night, thunderstorm—all were deified and adored as gods. But while being praised by the Vedic hymns, each of these gods was addressed or referred to as the Supreme God, the Lord of all gods, and the Creator of this universe. According to the famous German Indologist Max Müller, the earliest ancestors of the Hindus were, therefore, not polytheistic; they were henotheistic.[1]

Gradually the Indo-Aryan mind discovered some common ground behind this multiplicity of gods. The *Nāsadīya Hymn*,[2] or the "Creation Hymn" of the *Rig-Veda* tells us in beautiful and poetic language about a single primordial and extremely abstract principle designated *THAT*, from which the entire world has evolved. This principle is Pure Consciousness or Pure Spirit. It is

---

1. According to *Webster's New Universal Unabridged Dictionary*, henotheism means "(1) a religious doctrine attributing supreme power to one of several divinities in turn (2) belief in one god, without denying the existence of others."
2. Please see page 171.

65

beyond the world of space and time, beyond multiplicity, unfathomable and unknowable by ordinary human minds. That principle was there when neither the gods, nor men, nor anything else in creation existed. From that One and Only principle the world of Many has evolved. The Indo-Aryan genius at last arrived at the One and Only cause of everything, the One and Only God, who in Vedic Sanskrit is called *Brahman*. After that divine revelation the Vedic texts echoed the truth of the Oneness of Brahman again and again.

Vedic statements like *"Ekam sad viprā bahudhā vadanti"*[3]—"One alone exists, sages call It by various names," not only emphasize the oneness of God, but also form a firm foundation of catholicity and tolerance in Hinduism. The idea of harmony of religions is a fundamental ingredient of Hinduism.

The great sage Manu declared, "One ought to know the Supreme Spirit Who is the Ruler of all, subtler than the subtlest, of resplendent glory, and capable of being realized only by the meditation of pure-minded ones. Some call Him *Agni* (Fire); others call Him *Manu* (Thinker); and others *Prajāpati* (Lord of creatures). Some again call Him *Indra* (the Glorious); others *Prāna* (the Source of life); and still others the *Eternal Brahman* (the Great)."[4]

NIRGUNA BRAHMAN

If we ask, "Who was there before creation?" then the logical reply will be that only the creator, or God, was

---

3. *Rig-Veda* 1/164/46.
4. *Universal Prayers* (Madras, India: Sri Ramakrishna Math, 1933), xxxviii.

there. But if we ask, "What was God like *before* creation?" then Hinduism's reply will be that God was in a transcendental state of existence before creation. The word "transcendental" means that God's existence was beyond *our* time, space and causation. Hinduism holds that when God created the world he created time and space along with it. His pre-creation existence must, therefore, have been beyond time and space since they pertain only to this world.

To make this idea clear, let us take the help of an analogy. Let us consider a person who has fallen asleep and is dreaming. In his dream world, he exists in *dream* space and *dream* time, both of which he created with his mind when he created his dream world. He no longer belongs to the time and space of his *waking state*. In the dream state he has transcended the time and space of his waking state.

In the same manner, God's pre-creation existence must have been transcendental existence, because God then did not belong to the time and space pertaining to this world. God's existence in that state may be called the True State of the Existence of God. In that state God is beyond all limitations imposed by time, space and causation. God in that transcendental state is eternal, infinite and changeless.

In Hinduism, God in this transcendental state of existence is called *Nirguna Brahman*, the Supreme Spirit, the Supreme Brahman, or the Impersonal and Attributeless God.

Nirguna Brahman cannot have a personality. Personality is a limitation. Being devoid of a personality, Nirguna

Brahman is also beyond sex. Neither the pronoun "He" nor "She" can be used to denote Nirguna Brahman. The Vedas use the Sanskrit neuter pronoun *Tat*, the counterpart of the English word *That*, indicating that Nirguna Brahman is neither male nor female.

Transcending space, Nirguna Brahman is Infinite. Transcending time, Nirguna Brahman is Timeless or Eternal. Free from the ceaseless change generated by causation, Nirguna Brahman is Changeless.

Attribute or quality is a factor of separation. For example, the power of burning is a quality of fire. It separates fire from water, which lacks that quality. As Nirguna Brahman is One, Indivisible and Infinite, It cannot accommodate any kind of separation within Itself. Therefore, Nirguna Brahman must be attributeless, or free from all qualities.

Hinduism also uses the expressions "Absolute Truth," "Consciousness," and "Infinite Bliss" to mean Nirguna Brahman. But no matter what epithets are used, Nirguna Brahman can never be adequately described by the finite words and expressions of our world of limitations. Nirguna Brahman is indescribable. The great Hindu saint and philosopher Shankarāchārya says that Vedic statements such as *Sat-Chid-Ānandam*—"Brahman is Eternal Existence, Absolute Knowledge and Infinite Bliss"—are only hints about the nature of Nirguna Brahman. They are never the description of Nirguna Brahman.

ĪSHVARA

When man tries to think of the infinite Brahman with his finite mind, he unknowingly projects the limitations

Brahmā—The Creator

of his finite mind on Nirguna Brahman. As a result, Nirguna Brahman appears to become finite to him. The human mind can never think other than in human terms. It unknowingly projects human characteristics or qualities on Nirguna Brahman. Thus impersonal Nirguna Brahman acquires a personality very much resembling a human personality, no matter how glorified. Impersonal Nirguna Brahman appears to become Personal Brahman or Personal God. In reality Nirguna Brahman does not undergo any change or modification whatsoever. Personal God is no other than Impersonal God or Nirguna Brahman experienced through the veil of time, space and causation. It is like a person looking at the blue sky through three pairs of glasses, red, green and pink. When he uses his red glasses, the sky looks reddish; when he uses green glasses, the sky looks greenish; and when he looks through his pink glasses, the sky appears pinkish. In reality these colors are projected by the viewer's colored glasses on the sky. The sky does not change color at all. Similarly, the finite minds of people, like so many colored glasses, project their limitations on Nirguna Brahman. The changeless and infinite Nirguna Brahman appears to acquire limitations like personality. In reality

Nirguna Brahman does not undergo any change whatsoever. From Nirguna Brahman's standpoint Nirguna Brahman remains changeless. The idea of Personal God is therefore not the ultimate truth about God according to Hinduism. It is a relatively lower concept of God. Nevertheless, Personal God and Impersonal God are not essentially different from each other. Just as the reddish sky and the greenish sky are really the same sky, so also Personal God is no other than Impersonal God. They are essentially one and the same.

Personal God in Hinduism is called *Saguna Brahman* or *Īshvara*. From the standpoint of man posited in the world of time, space and causation, Īshvara or Saguna Brahman is the creator of this world. He is omnipotent, omniscient and all-pervading. By His mere will He manifests Himself as the manifold universe. Although formless, by His divine magical power, *Māyā*, He assumes various forms. By His māyā He has created the world with good and evil in it.[5] Even though the world is in Him, He is beyond the good and evil of the world. He is like a cobra, which is not affected by the poison in its mouth. Its poison affects others only.

Īshvara is not only the creator, but the preserver and destroyer as well. Creation, preservation and destruction go hand in hand in this world. Īshvara, therefore, has three basic aspects: (1) the creator aspect, (2) the preserver aspect and (3) the destroyer aspect. These three

---

5. According to the Vishishtādvaita school of Vedānta philosophy, Īshvara has six divine qualities: (i) Jnāna (infinite knowledge), (ii) Bala (infinite strength), (iii) Aishwarya (lordship over everything), (iv) Shakti (creative power), (v) Vīrya (infinite vigor), and (vi) Tejas (majestic luster).

Vishnu—The Preserver

basic aspects of Īshvara are given the names Brahmā, Vishnu and Shiva respectively. When Īshvara creates, He is called Brahmā; when He preserves, He is called Vishnu; and when He destroys, He is called Shiva.

Īshvara is sexless. Yet the Hindus can look upon Īshvara as both father and mother. According to the devotees' mental attitudes they can establish other relationships with Īshvara as well. They can look upon Īshvara as friend, child, or even husband or sweetheart, for such relationships are nothing but mental projections on Īshvara. Many great women saints of Hinduism considered themselves to be spiritually married to God. They looked upon God as their Divine Husband or Divine Sweetheart. Some women saints looked upon God as their Divine Child. Many saints of Hinduism like Kamalākānta, Rāmprasād, Shrī Rāmakrishna and others looked upon God as the Divine Mother. Such relationships were purely mental and completely devoid of any kind of association with the physical body.

Shiva—The Destroyer

According to Shrī Rāmakrishna, the famous 19th century saint of India, such attitudes toward God can generate feelings of great closeness between God and the devotees, and thus hasten God-realization.

Īshvara is also the originator and upholder of the eternal moral order in this world. This moral order or basic law, which is called *Rita* in Sanskrit, maintains the regularity and orderliness of everything in this universe including the stars and planets.

DEITIES IN HINDUISM

Aside from the three basic aspects, Īshvara has endless powers or aspects. One or more of these aspects can be personified as a deity in Hinduism. For instance, when a Hindu thinks of Īshvara as the giver of knowledge and learning, that aspect of Īshvara is personified as the deity *Sarasvatī*. In the same manner, the deity *Lakshmī* personifies Īshvara as the giver of wealth and prosperity.

It should be clearly understood that the deities are not so many different gods, they are the personifications of various aspects of one and the same Īshvara.

DEVAS AND DEVĪS: BEINGS WITH SHINING BODIES

Certain created beings who have done a lot of meritorious work while on earth are promoted after their death to hold various exalted positions. These exalted beings acquire special bodies which give out light. The Sanskrit word *div* means "to shine." These beings, therefore, are called *Devas* (masculine) or *Devīs* (feminine) depending upon whether they are male or female.

The greatest of the Devas is Hiranyagarbha, who has infinite powers. He was the first being created by God (Īshvara). Even though a created being, Hiranyagarbha has almost God-like powers. He is Cosmic Intelligence. By Īshvara's will, Hiranyagarbha created this world. Hiranyagarbha is the first manifestation of God (Īshvara), therefore, he deserves the adoration of all. All other Devas and Devīs exist in Hiranyagarbha, because Hiranyagarbha is infinite and comprises the entire world. Adoration of any one of them, therefore, is like adoring Hiranyagarbha himself. Sometimes the Purānas deify Hiranyagarbha and raise him to the level of Īshvara. Then he is called Brahmā, the creator.

Except for Hiranyagarbha, these beings are not spiritually illumined or liberated souls. They acquire exalted positions as a result of their meritorious deeds done on earth. When the effect of their meritorious deeds is worn out they have to be born again as human beings.

PRESIDING DEVAS OR DEVĪS

Hinduism speaks of presiding Devas or Devīs—in Sanskrit, *Adhishthātri Deva* and *Adhishthātrī Devī*—who control various animate and inanimate domains of this universe. These domains can be either subtle or gross, or very large or small. For example, Indra is the presiding Deva or the controller of the arms and hands of all people. Similarly, Hiranyagarbha is the presiding Deva of the sum total of all individual minds in this universe. Or, in other words, Hiranyagarbha considers the sum total of all minds as his own mind. In the same way, the presiding Deva of the sum total of all material bodies in this universe is Virāt. Virāt considers the entire material universe as his own body. To explain, let us consider a human body. A body is like a skin-bound universe for all the minute life forms existing in it. We also know that a human body has white blood corpuscles. They seem to have a keen sense of duty to protect the body from harmful intruders. As soon as some germs enter the body, the white blood corpuscles attack them. Had it been possible for someone to talk to a white blood corpuscle and say, "Look, you live in a skin-bound universe. There is a being who thinks that this universe is his body. He is the presiding Deva of your universe." Then the white blood corpuscle would most probably say, "Are you kidding?"

We are very much like that white blood corpuscle. Our mental conditioning makes it hard for us to accept the idea of a presiding Deva or Devī, but it will not be prudent to dismiss the idea as ridiculous. If we are unbiased, we have to admit that the existence of such beings is not impossible. Hinduism asserts that such beings do exist.

DIVINE INCARNATIONS

According to Hinduism, when religion declines and irreligion prevails, God out of His compassion incarnates on earth to revitalize religion. Then He is called a Divine Incarnation, or *Avatāra* in Sanskrit. Since the beginning of creation God has incarnated many times and He will again do so in the future whenever such necessity arises. The first few times God incarnated in the form of subhuman beings. He incarnated first as a fish, then as a turtle, and after that as a boar. Then He incarnated as a combination of beast and man.[6] All His subsequent incarnations were in human form.

Science tells us that early life forms on earth were fish or aquatic animals. Then came amphibians such as turtles. They were followed by land animals like boars. After them the first ancestors of man made their appearance. They were not quite human; they were a combination of both man and animal. Gradually they evolved into human beings. The resemblance between the Divine Incarnations of the earlier period and evolving life forms on earth is indeed quite striking.

---

6. God incarnated as "Nrisimha"—half man and half lion.

Shrī Krishna

One may wonder why God incarnated in forms other than human. To explain this, Hinduism draws our attention to the fact that all creatures were created by one and the same compassionate God. God's infinite compassion, which causes His descent on earth as a Divine Incarnation, should be the same for both human and subhuman beings. Otherwise God becomes biased and partial, an idea which is not acceptable.

A Paurānic scripture of Hinduism, the *Shrīmad Bhāgavata*, mentions the possibility of innumerable Divine Incarnations. Some other scriptures mention only ten.[7]

The Vedas, however, do not speak of Divine Incarnations. They speak of the *Rishis* or sages. But not all sages were of the same spiritual caliber; a few of them outshone the others in their spiritual attainments. In a later period when the different schools of Hindu philosophy were developed, these exalted sages came to be known as *Adhikārī Purushas*—persons endowed with superhuman

---

7. These are the ten Divine Incarnations: (1) Matsya, (2) Kūrma, (3) Varāha, (4) Nrisimha, (5) Vāmana, (6) Parashurāma, (7) Rāma, (8a) Balarāma/(8b) Krishnā, (9) Buddha and (10) Kalki. Both Balarāma and Krishna are considered the 8th Divine Incarnation; if we count both of them, the number comes to eleven.

power or authority. The Adhikārī Purushas, though human, could not be put in the category of other human beings because they were extraordinary. Sānkhya, the most ancient school of Hindu religious philosophy, would call an Adhikārī Purusha *Īshvarakoti* or *Kalpaniyāmaka Īshvara*.

The phenomenon of a Divine Incarnation has always been present, but was not interpreted correctly during the Vedic period or when the Sānkhya or other schools of philosophy were developed in India. Only in the much later Paurānic period was the phenomenon correctly interpreted. The post-Vedic Adhikārī Purusha, Īshvarakoti, or Kalpaniyāmaka Īshvara was no other than the Divine Incarnation of the Paurānic period. This is the view of some Hindu scholars.[8]

God incarnates on earth to fulfill two purposes: (1) to inspire and (2) to liberate. He inspires mankind through example. He willingly takes upon Himself human limitations. Then through intense spiritual practice He goes beyond them and manifests His spiritual perfection. It should be understood here that as He is perfect from His very birth, the Divine Incarnation does not really need any spiritual practice to attain perfection. Nevertheless, to inspire others He goes through various spiritual disciplines and thereby manifests His perfection to set an example for mankind. Just as a hen, which itself is not hungry, may pick at and gobble up birdseed to teach its young ones how to eat, so also a Divine Incarnation, for

---

8. See *Shrī Rāmakrishna The Great Master*—a translation by Swamī Jagadānanda of the Bengali original named *Shrī Shrī Rāmakrishna Līlāprasanga* by Swamī Sāradānanda.

the sake of mankind, goes through various spiritual austerities in order to teach them how to attain perfection through spiritual practice.

The Divine Incarnation liberates from their sins those who completely surrender to Him, and helps them attain perfection. Shrī Krishna, a Divine Incarnation, says in the *Bhagavad Gītā*, "Abandoning all rites and duties take refuge in me alone. Do not grieve; for I shall liberate you from all sins."[9]

---

9. *Bhagavad Gītā* 18/66.

IX

THE DOCTRINE OF KARMA

INTRODUCTION

Hinduism believes in the doctrine of cause and effect, which in Sanskrit is called *Karmavāda*—the theory or doctrine of karma. The word *karma* means action. Sometimes the word is also used to mean the effect of action. According to this doctrine, all good actions produce good effects, and bad actions bad. The effects or fruits of action are generally called *karmaphala*[1] in Sanskrit. The fruits of good deeds bring pleasure and enjoyment to the doer, while the fruits of bad deeds cause him suffering and pain.

Physics tells us about the theory of conservation of energy. According to this theory, energy is never destroyed; rather, one kind of energy becomes transformed into another kind of energy. Using this idea as an analogy, it can be said that energy expended through any action of the doer only changes its form and becomes karmic force or karmaphala. This force, like a boomerang, inevitably comes back to the doer sooner or later. Returning to the doer the karmic force starts acting on his mind and body causing either pleasure or pain. No doer can escape this karmic force. After working on the mind and

---

1. Sanskrit: *karma* = work; *phala* = fruit.

body of the doer, the karmic force is spent. It leaves the doer and becomes a part of the vast storehouse of cosmic energy.

According to this doctrine, God is not responsible for the pleasure or pain of His creatures. It is the creatures who are responsible for their own enjoyment or suffering. They suffer or enjoy owing to the consequences of their own bad or good deeds. According to Hinduism, God is *karmaphaladātā*—the giver of the fruits of action. He is the ultimate dispenser of justice. He makes sure that everyone gets his own karmaphala, not someone else's.

During an average lifetime a doer performs innumerable deeds, the effects of which are equally countless. All the effects of his actions do not immediately return to him, although some of them may. For instance, if a person plants an apple sapling in his orchard it will be years before he can get the fruits. But if he puts his hand into fire it will have immediate effect; his hand will be burnt.

SANCHITA KARMA AND PRĀRABDHA KARMA

Some actions, owing to their inherent nature, yield late effects. They are like term deposits with late maturity dates. Some may mature years from now. Similarly, the late-bearing fruits of some actions may not come during the doer's lifetime. Such fruits of action or karmaphala will remain stored up until their "maturity" dates. They may come in a future lifetime of the doer. Thus, in Hinduism, the doctrine of karma is also tied in with the doctrine of reincarnation.

Stored up karmic forces are the effect of the deeds done

by the doer in his past lives. These forces are called
sanchita karma or accumulated karmic forces. They
remain in a potential state like so many term deposits
with different maturity dates in a bank. When one
matures, it becomes kinetic and starts acting on the mind
and body of the doer. The karmic force in this kinetic
form is called *prārabdha karma*—the karmic force which
has started yielding effect. According to Hinduism,
prārabdha karma causes a person's birth and determines
how long he will live. It also causes pleasure or pain during the lifetime of a person. When the force of his prārabdha karma is exhausted, his body dies. It is as though the
body is a clock, the main spring of which has been
wound up by the prārabdha karma to go on ticking for a
certain number of years. When that energy is used up the
clock stops.

KRIYAMĀNA (ĀGĀMĪ) KARMA

Any action done in this life, or its effect, is called
kriyamāna karma or *āgāmī karma* in Sanskrit. The Hindu
scriptures tell us which kind of kriyamāna karma or
action done in this life will yield immediate effect. A person who has committed extremely heinous crimes,[2] like
killing a saintly soul or a woman, will suffer from their
bad effects in this very life. Other good or bad actions,
which are relatively trivial, may not yield immediate
effects. These actions go on accumulating during a person's lifetime as kriyamāna karma and eventually join the
vast storehouse of sanchita or accumulated karma.

---

2. In Sanskrit, *atyutkata karma*.

HINDUISM'S VIEW ON SUICIDE

If a person stops his "body clock" prematurely by committing suicide, he commits a great mistake. His karmic force does not stop with his death. It goes on hounding him even in the other world. For this unnatural death caused by himself, the karmic force inflicts many times more suffering and pain on him than what he would have suffered had he been alive. Therefore, Hinduism very strongly condemns suicide.

HINDUISM'S INTERPRETATION OF DEATH IN CHILDHOOD

In the light of reincarnation, Hinduism does not necessarily consider a newborn child to be a "pure" or an "innocent" soul. Nor does Hinduism believe that a child who dies shortly after birth goes to heaven or becomes liberated. Every birth is an opportunity for an individual to grow and progress spiritually through the bitter and sweet experiences of life. Those dying in infancy do not get that opportunity. A person with a lot of bad karma to work out may be repeatedly born just in order to die again and again in his infancy. He works out his bad karma by going through the painful process of repeated and fruitless births and deaths. The short duration of his life on earth prevents him from making any spiritual progress.

CAN A SAINT HAVE PHYSICAL ILLNESS OR MENTAL SUFFERING?

There is a wrong notion in some people's minds that a real saint must not suffer any physical illness or mental pain. Their notion is based on the supposition that the saint, being perfect, must not suffer like other people. But many genuine saints have been seen to go through a lot of physical and mental suffering in their lives. The saying, "A saint has a past, and a sinner a future," may explain why a saint suffers in this life. The saint must have done some bad deeds in one or more of his past lives. He is working out the effect of those deeds in this life in the form of physical or mental suffering. Even though spiritually illumined now, he still must work out his prārabdha karma until the force of that karma is exhausted.[3]

According to the doctrine of karma, when a person becomes a saint by having the ultimate spiritual experience, all his sanchita or accumulated karma is, as it were, burnt to ashes. But he cannot get rid of his prārabdha karma until his death.

Hinduism uses a beautiful analogy to explain this. A hunter has his quiver full of arrows. These arrows are his sanchita or "accumulated" karma. He takes an arrow from his quiver, puts it in his bow, and shoots it. The arrow shot by him is his prārabdha karma. Once the arrow is released from his bow he does not have any more control over it. It keeps on going through the air and drops to the ground when its energy is completely exhausted. Prārabdha karma is like the arrow over which the hunter does not have any more control. Prārabdha karma creates a man's body and goes on bringing

---

3. In the context of Hinduism, a saint is one who has experienced God face to face in this life. It may also be said that a saint is one who has attained perfection by manifesting his or her inherent divinity.

pleasure and pain until all its karmic force is exhausted, and then the body dies. Even saints are not exempted from this process.

A DIVINE INCARNATION IS BEYOND
THE KARMIC FORCES

There is, however, an exception to this rule. A Divine Incarnation is never controlled by the forces of karma, nor is his body caused by any prārabdha karma. God, in order to incarnate on earth in human form, creates an earthly body for Himself through His inscrutable magical power or māyā and enters into it. By His māyā He gives others the impression that He is born of human parents. Out of compassion for His creatures who take refuge in Him, He absorbs their sins or bad karma in His earthly body, and suffers on their behalf. He works out their bad prārabdha karma to give them relief and salvation. Neither does a Divine Incarnation generate any karmaphala for whatever he does during his earthly existence.

SUFFERING AT BIRTH—SEEN IN THE
LIGHT OF KARMA & REINCARNATION

Why one child is born blind while another is born with a perfect body cannot be explained by saying that it happens according to God's will. In that case God would be either biased or whimsical. Hinduism explains this disparity in terms of both reincarnation and the doctrine of karma. The child has been born blind as the result of bad deeds done in some previous incarnations. The stored up karmaphala of the past births has taken effect as blindness in this birth.

KARMIC FORCES DO NOT
COMPLETELY GOVERN HUMAN LIVES

It should be clearly understood that Hinduism never says that everything that happens in a person's life is the result of his actions from previous births. Karmic force is just one of the many forces which control his life. In spite of these forces working on him, he has quite a bit of freedom of action as well. He should exercise this freedom by acting in a manner which will spare him suffering or pain in the future and help him to attain liberation through the realization of God.

The scriptures of Hinduism, the *Bhagavad Gītā* in particular, also tell us that a person can get rid of all his karmic forces, except those of prārabdha karma, if he performs his activities without expecting the fruits of his own actions. A devotee of God is encouraged to develop the attitude that his actions are not for his own sake but for the pleasure of God. Work done with this attitude helps him to become free from the late-bearing effects of actions (kriyamāna karma) done in this life. It also purifies his mind and thereby enables him to have the vision of God. After God vision he gets rid of all his sanchita or accumulated karma. Thus he attains liberation from the cycle of repeated births and deaths. Nevertheless, he has to work out his prārabdha karma, from the grip of which no mortal can completely escape. Some say, however, that even though one cannot completely escape from one's prārabdha karma, the intensity of its forces can be considerably reduced if one surrenders to God completely. Shrī Sāradā Devī (1853-1920), one of the greatest women saints of India, supports this view. She says, "By surrendering to God a devotee can considerably reduce his prārabdha karma. For instance, had he been fated to have a sword injury owing to his karmic forces, he will have a pin-prick instead."

GOD'S GRACE IN HINDUISM

In the light of the doctrine of karma it may seem that man is responsible for whatever happens to him in his life in the form of pleasure or pain. Since God is only the giver of man's karmaphala, His role is no different from the role of a cashier in a bank. The cashier cannot give any money to the depositor other than his invested capital and its interest. Where then is the scope for God's grace in Hinduism?

In reply, Hinduism says that God's grace cannot be conditional. Any conditional gift cannot be called real grace. Therefore, God's grace has to be unconditional, unbiased and impartial. Just as the sun shines on both the good and the wicked, so also God showers His grace impartially on everyone, whether good or evil. The good use God's grace for good purposes. The wicked use God's grace for bad purposes.

Shrī Rāmakrishna explains this with the help of a beautiful analogy. In a small room a candle is burning. By the light of the candle one person is reading a holy book, while another person in the same room is forging dollar bills. In this analogy the candlelight represents God's grace. It is impartial; it shines equally on both. The two persons are using God's grace for two completely different purposes—one good, and the other bad. Perhaps one of them will eventually turn into a saint, while the other will end up in prison.

According to Shrī Rāmakrishna the breeze of God's grace is always blowing. Everyone in this world is like the owner of a sailboat. As long as the sail of the boat is not unfurled one cannot take advantage of the breeze—one cannot get the benefit of God's grace. But as soon as the sail is unfurled, the breeze of divine grace starts moving the boat. In this analogy the act of unfurling the sail is no other than making self-effort. Without self-effort one will neither be able to appreciate nor enjoy the benefit of God's grace.

X

THE DOCTRINE OF PREDESTINATION

According to the doctrine of predestination, every event in the life of an individual has already been determined by God—everything happens only according to God's will. Individuals do not have any control over events. In the light of the doctrine of predestination the doctrine of karma cannot be accepted as a valid doctrine, and vice versa.

Hinduism, however, accepts both of these doctrines as valid. According to Hinduism, the doctrine of karma is valid for a person who has the sense of agency or doership. Such a person holds himself responsible for his actions, whether good or bad. But through intense spiritual practice a spiritual aspirant's mind can be made to acquire higher and higher degrees of purity. At a certain high level of mental purity the spiritual aspirant completely loses his sense of agency. He gains the firm conviction that he is not the doer of any of his actions. He becomes convinced that God has been doing everything by using his body, mind, energy and the senses. He feels that he is only an instrument in the hands of God, and whatever God has been doing to him is for his ultimate spiritual good. At this high level of spirituality the doctrine of predestination becomes the only valid doctrine to him. To him the doctrine of karma ceases to be a valid doctrine.

Therefore, these two doctrines, even though apparently contradictory to each other, are valid for people at different stages of spiritual growth. At an intermediate level of spiritual growth, however, a spiritual aspirant may interpret some events of his life in terms of the doctrine of predestination while he may interpret other events of his life in terms of the doctrine of karma.

XI

THE DOCTRINE OF REINCARNATION

INTRODUCTION

The idea of reincarnation in Hinduism is perhaps as old as Hinduism itself. To students of religion reincarnation is a theological doctrine. Most Hindus consider it a fact. The evidence in support of reincarnation comes from two sources: (1) *Jātismaras*—people who can remember their past birth or births and (2) the testimony of the scriptures or saints.

Hindu religious literature is full of numerous references to reincarnation. In the *Bhagavad Gītā*, Shrī Krishna, a Divine Incarnation, says to his student Arjuna, "Arjuna, both you and I were born many times in the past. You do not remember those births, but I remember them all." In this particular context Shrī Krishna can be called a jātismara, a person who remembers his past births, but Arjuna is not.

Hinduism believes that not only the Divine Incarnations like Shrī Krishna, but pure-minded saints also, if they want to, can remember their past incarnations. Through the years some people who are neither divine incarnations nor saints have also displayed the rare ability to remember their past lives. Their number is quite small. Nevertheless, the validity of many such cases has been proved in India through reliable and unbiased investigations throughout the ages.

The doctrine of reincarnation explains many things which cannot otherwise be explained adequately. For instance, the genius of a child prodigy like Mozart cannot be satisfactorily explained by heredity or genes alone. Only the doctrine of reincarnation can explain this satisfactorily. Such a prodigy must have been a highly accomplished musician in his last birth, and he carried that talent over to this incarnation.

In reply to the question, "Why does a person reincarnate?" Hinduism says that the unfulfilled desires of departed people are primarily responsible for their rebirth. To understand this position one should know Hinduism's view about death and thereafter.

THE GROSS AND SUBTLE BODIES OF MAN

According to Hinduism, man has two bodies, the gross and the subtle. The gross body is the physical body. The subtle body consists of the mind, intellect, sense organs, motor organs and vital energy. The physical eyes, ears, nose, tongue and skin are not considered real sense organs. They are only offices used by the senses of sight, hearing, smell, taste and touch to establish contact with the external world. The real sense organs are extremely subtle.

DEATH AND THE LOKAS—THE DIFFERENT PLANES OF EXISTENCE

When a person dies, his gross physical body is left behind and the soul with the subtle body, consisting of his mind, intellect, vital energy and his motor and sense organs, goes to a different plane of existence. Such a plane of existence is called a *loka* in Sanskrit.[1] In addition to this earthly plane, which is called *Bhūrloka*, there are innumerable lokas. They are worlds of different sets of vibrations. All of them, however, occupy the same space. The lokas are neither above nor below in relation to this earthly plane. They have the same spatial existence.

It is not possible for anyone to produce an exhaustive list of the lokas because they are innumerable. Nevertheless, Hinduism speaks of fourteen lokas[2] including this earthly plane (*Bhūrloka*). The lokas are *Satyaloka, Tapoloka, Maharloka, Janaloka, Svarloka, Bhuvarloka, Bhūrloka, Atalaloka, Vitalaloka, Sutalaloka, Rasātalaloka, Talātalaloka, Mahātalaloka* and *Pātālaloka*. Among these lokas the first six are considered the higher lokas[3] and the last seven are considered the lower lokas. The adjectives higher or lower in this context are used in comparison to conditions found in *Bhūrloka*. In the higher lokas, in ascending order, there is more and more enjoyment or spiritual bliss compared to what is usually found on this earthly plane. Similarly, in the lower lokas, in descending order, there is more and more suffering. All these joys or sufferings, however, are experienced by the departed soul

---

1. According to popular concept there are three lokas. They are *Svarga, Martya* and *Pātāla,* but the scriptures speak of many more.
2. Swāmī Nikhilānanda, *Vedāntasāra of Sadānanda* (Calcutta: Advaita Ashrama, 1978), 61.
3. Scriptures of Hinduism mention other higher lokas also. *Kaushītaki Upanishad* (1.3) mentions *Brahmaloka, Prajāpatiloka, Indraloka, Ādityaloka, Varunaloka, Vāyuloka* and *Agniloka* as the seven higher lokas.

only through his mind. The degree of purity of his mind determines where his soul along with his subtle body will go. A departed soul goes to a higher loka if his mind is pure, and to a relatively lower loka if it is not. As determined by his past karma, the departed soul remains in one of these lokas for a certain period of time, either suffering or enjoying there.

UNFULFILLED DESIRE CAUSES REINCARNATION

When a person dies with a strong unfulfilled desire which can only be fulfilled on earth, his mind—while he is in the other world—strongly yearns for the fulfillment of that desire. That unfulfilled desire eventually brings him back to earth, thus causing his rebirth or reincarnation. An analogy will explain this more clearly. Let us suppose a person is extremely fond of a special exotic dish which is served by an exclusive restaurant in the city where he lives. But the restaurant is ten miles away from his home. One day he develops a great craving for that dish. His strong desire to enjoy that dish persuades him to get into his car and drive ten miles to that restaurant. So also the urge of the departed soul to satisfy his unfulfilled desire will bring him back to earth until his desire is fulfilled.

REINCARNATION—AN OPPORTUNITY TO MAKE SPIRITUAL PROGRESS

Reincarnation also gives a person the opportunity to gradually evolve spiritually through the various valuable experiences he acquires in his different incarnations. Eventually he reaches the acme of his spiritual progress through God-realization. After realizing God he goes beyond all desires because he no longer lacks anything. He transcends the chain of repeated births and deaths. Such a person is called a liberated soul.

TRANSMIGRATION OF SOULS

The idea of the transmigration of souls is also present in Hinduism. Generally speaking, a human soul goes on evolving from incarnation to incarnation. It is normal for a human soul to be born again and again only in human bodies until he is liberated. But there may be rare exceptions. In these exceptional cases a human soul may be born once or twice in a subhuman body to work out very bad Karma. When the bad Karma is worked out, the soul incarnates again in a human body and goes through the process of gradual spiritual evolution.

REINCARNATION AND THE IDEA OF EVOLUTION OF SPECIES

Those who do not accept the idea of reincarnation sometimes argue that the total number of human beings should have been depleted because so many human beings must have been liberated from death and rebirth since the beginning of creation. But Hinduism refutes this objection by stating that many subhuman beings through the course of evolution are being born as human beings. Consequently, the number of human beings is increasing. Hinduism also asserts that divinity is equally present in every soul, whether that be in a human or a subhuman body. Otherwise it goes against the idea of God's omnipresence.

Patanjali, the founder of the Yoga system of philosophy, speaks of the transformation of one genus or species into another. In Sanskrit it is called *jātyantara-parināma*. According to Patanjali, one genus or species potentially has the ability to evolve into another genus or species when changing circumstances create a suitable environment for such evolution.

XII

HINDU ETHICS

INTRODUCTION

The foundation of Hindu ethics is the Vedic teaching that God (Brahman) and the indwelling Self of man are one and the same. Behind the psychophysical man is the Self, which is divine. *Ayam ātmā Brahma*—"This Self is Brahman," is a fundamental teaching of the Hindu scriptures.

The Self forms the very core of man's being. It is different from his physical body, vital energy, senses and mind. Man's ego is not this Self. The ego or I-ness is an idea only; it is purely mental. Being mental, it cannot be the Self. This Self of man is called *Ātman* in Sanskrit.

If Brahman is compared to an infinite ocean, then Ātman is a wave in it. The ocean is never different from its waves, and the waves are never different from the ocean. They are one and the same. Thus, Brahman and Ātman are one and the same. It is Ātman which has become the manifold universe. If I hurt anyone, I actually hurt myself. Therefore, I must not hurt anyone. This realization is the basis of Hindu ethics.

The *Īsha Upanishad* says very beautifully, "He who sees all beings in the Self, and the Self in all beings, hates no one." It is possible for us to hate others only when that awareness of unity is not there. In the *Brihadāranyaka Upanishad* there is a dialogue between the sage, Yājnavalkya, and his virtuous wife, Maitreyī. In that dialogue Yājnavalkya says that our awareness of the presence of the Self in all makes everyone dear to us. The spiritual goal of Hinduism is to experience this divine Self within and without.

DHARMA OR RELIGIOUS DUTIES

The word *dharma* plays a very important role in Hindu ethics. *Dharma* usually means religion. It also means moral and ethical duty. One definition of dharma says, "Dhārayati dharma ity-āhu"—"Whatever sustains is dharma."[1] The Divine Self is the very foundation of our being, and it is that which sustains us. Therefore, according to this definition, the highest meaning of the word dharma is the Divine Self in man, the Ātman.

However, in regard to the day-to-day practice of morality and ethics, dharma has a relatively lower meaning in Hinduism. In mundane life there are different types of dharma, such as *vyakti-dharma* or the dharma of an individual, *pārivārika-dharma* or family-dharma, *samāja-dharma* or society-dharma, *rāshtra-dharma* or national dharma, and *mānava-dharma* or the dharma of mankind.

The observance of moral and ethical principles sustains an individual's mind. Following the rules of health and hygiene sustains his physical body. Such observances at the individual level constitute vyakti-dharma. There are

---

1. Also *"Prithivīm dharmanā dhritam"*—"The world is sustained by dharma." *Atharva Veda* 12/1/17.

also other observances, listed below, which also come
under the category of vyakti-dharma:[2]

- *Dama*—control of the external organs
- *Ārjava*—straightforwardness at all times
- *Ahimsā*—abstention from injury to all forms
  of life
- *Akrodha*—absence of anger
- *Satya*—truthfulness in thought and speech
- *Brahmacharya*—control of carnal desires and
  passions
- *Santosha*—contentment
- *Tyāga*—renunciation of selfishness
- *Apaishuna*—refraining from vilification and
  backbiting
- *Aloluptva*—non-covetousness
- *Aparigraha*—non-acceptance of unnecessary
  gifts from others
- *Hrī*—modesty
- *Mārdava*—gentleness
- *Dayā*—kindness and compassion
- *Shānti*—peace of mind attained through its
  control
- *Kshamā*—forgiveness
- *Shaucha*—purification of body and mind
- *Adroha*—freedom from malice.

Individuals make up a family. For the well-being of the
individual the family has to be sustained. Codes of conduct to be observed by individuals to prevent the disinte-
gration of the family are pārivārika-dharma or family-
dharma. The basis of family-dharma is mutual self-
sacrifice and respect. Upanishadic statements such as

---

2. See *The Bhagavad Gītā* 16/1, 2 & 3. Also read *Yoga Sūtras Of Patanjali* 2/30.

"Treat your mother as a god" and "Treat your father as a god,"[3] are included in the codes of family-dharma. If families do not survive, individuals cannot survive.

Families make up a society. If society disintegrates, families cannot survive. Therefore, individuals must observe codes of conduct to maintain a well-integrated society. This is samāja-dharma or society-dharma. Self-sacrifice of various kinds made for the sustenance of society is the basis of society-dharma. The practice of nonviolence, non-stealing, truthfulness, refraining from speaking a truth which hurts, control of anger, control of the lower passions, practicing charity and kindness to all, refraining from backbiting, practicing hospitality, etc., constitute samāja-dharma.

If the nation disintegrates, society cannot survive. Individuals have to make some self-sacrifice for their country also in order to sustain its existence. This is rāshtra-dharma or national-dharma.

If mankind does not survive, it is impossible for nations to survive. Individuals, therefore, have to behave in a manner which will be conducive to the sustenance of mankind. This behavior comes under the category of mānava-dharma. It also consists of self-sacrifice.

All these dharmas are like so many concentric circles at the center of which is the individual, who is performing the dharmas. An ideal Hindu is supposed to observe all these dharmas. It is a hard task, but pursuing a high ideal alone can make life noble and meaningful. Self-sacrifice is the common denominator among all these dharmas.

---

3. See *Taittirīya Upanishad* 1/11/2.

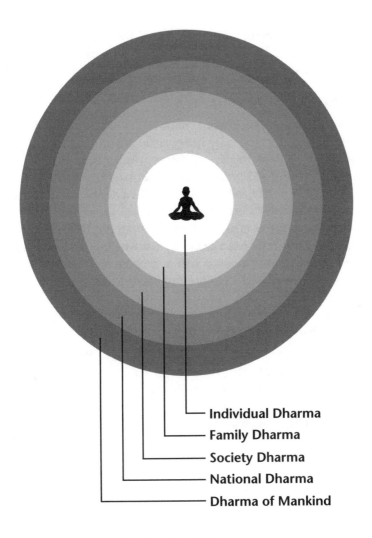

Individual Dharma
Family Dharma
Society Dharma
National Dharma
Dharma of Mankind

The Levels of Dharma

Without self-sacrifice the survival of the individual is not possible. Such self-sacrifice is in fact self-sustenance and self-preservation; it is not self-deprivation.

FIVE DEBTS OR PANCHA RINA

According to Hinduism, man has five debts: (1) *deva-rina* or debt to God, (2) *rishi-rina* or debt to the sages, (3) *pitri-rina* or debt to the ancestors, (4) *nri-rina* or debt to mankind and (5) *bhūta-rina* or debt to the subhuman beings. A Hindu has to repay these five debts through the performance of certain moral duties enjoined by the scriptures. Hindu ethics believes that all life forms belong to one ecosystem. Man cannot exist without acknowledging his indebtedness to other human beings and life forms on earth. All lives are interdependent. One cannot survive without the survival of others. Wanton destruction of life, whether human or subhuman, is not permitted by Hinduism.

One of the scriptures of Hinduism says that a Hindu has to maintain ethical behavior from his inception in his mother's womb until his death.[4]

GOD IS THE UPHOLDER
OF MORALITY

The Vedas also declare God to be the creator and upholder of *rita*, the eternal moral order. The entire universe is controlled by *rita*. All laws which maintain the orderliness of this universe and the other subtler worlds

---

4. *"Nishekādi shmashānantah"*—"Starting from the inception in one's mother's womb and ending in the cremation ground." *Agniveshya Grihyasutra* 3/10/4.

are included in rita. None in this universe can escape this moral law. Therefore, Hinduism considers God to be the very foundation of ethics and morality.

XIII

GURU AND DISCIPLE RELATIONSHIP

In Hindu tradition a teacher, whether he gives spiritual or secular education, is worthy of great respect. The spiritual teacher, who is called a *guru*, is given the greatest respect and veneration by a student. The word "guru" means "the dispeller of spiritual darkness."[1] The word "guru" can also be used to mean a teacher of secular education.

A spiritual aspirant must have *shraddhā* for his guru. In the present context the Sanskrit word *shraddhā* has two meanings: (1) self confidence and (2) implicit faith in the words of the guru. The *Bhagavad Gītā* says, "One who has shraddhā attains knowledge,"[2] meaning that a student must have the confidence that when guided by his teacher he will be able to succeed. He should also have implicit faith in the teachings of his teacher.

Various Upanishads, epics and legends stress the necessity for shraddhā. The *Chhāndogya Upanishad* tells a story of Satyakāma to illustrate this. As a boy, Satyakāma went to his teacher's home to live and study. But his teacher Gautama did not give him any lessons. Instead, he gave Satyakāma four hundred lean and sickly cows and asked him to take care of them. Satyakāma had shraddhā; he had implicit faith in his guru. Happily obeying the order

---

1. *Guru Gītā* 20.
2. *Bhagavad Gītā* 4/39.

of his teacher, the boy drove the cattle toward the forest. He lived in the forest for many years caring for the cattle until their number increased to a thousand.

Then strange things started happening. The bull of the herd approached Satyakāma and, speaking in human language, reminded him to take the cattle back to his teacher's home. The bull also gave Satyakāma teachings about Brahman (God). On his way back Satyakāma was given more teachings about Brahman by a fire which he lit one evening. Thereafter a swan and a loon also gave Satyakāma similar teachings.

At last the boy arrived at his teacher's home. As soon as Gautama set his eyes upon Satyakāma he said, "My son, your face shines like one who is a knower of Brahman. Please tell me who taught you." The boy replied, "I have been taught by beings other than men. But I also want you to teach me, because I have heard that the teachings of one's own guru alone can lead a student to the supreme good." Then the sage Gautama imparted to Satyakāma the same knowledge which the boy had acquired from nonhuman sources. This story gives the message that the highest knowledge comes to a student who has shraddhā for his teacher.

The great epic *Mahābhārata* has a similar story about an outcaste Nishāda[3] boy, Ekalavya, who wanted to learn archery from Drona, one of the greatest Aryan teachers of martial art in ancient India. As it was against the custom

---

3. According to the Law Book of Manu, a Nishāda is the child of a Brahmin father and a Shūdra mother and, thus, an outcaste. Some scholars, however, hold that Nishādas were non-Aryan. Ekalavya's father was king of a Nishāda tribe.

of the Aryans to teach the secrets of warfare to outcastes, Drona refused to accept Ekalavya as his student. Nevertheless, Ekalavya mentally accepted Drona as his teacher. He built a statue of Drona in the forest, and with intense shraddhā for his guru started practicing archery without anybody's help in front of that statue. After a few years, by virtue of his shraddhā, Ekalavya became such a great archer that he even excelled Prince Arjuna, who was the best student of Drona.

Not everyone can be a guru. Only a person with an exemplary life and high spiritual attainments can be a guru. Otherwise, he will not be able to help a student. The student has to follow the instructions of the teacher and sincerely strive to reach the goal of his spiritual life.

A true spiritual teacher must never charge any money for the guidance that he gives his student. A teacher who violates this sacred time-honored tradition of Hinduism brings only disgrace to himself and his religion.

XIV

TWO DIFFERENT SPIRITUAL PATHS

INTRODUCTION

As has been mentioned earlier, the ultimate goal of human life according to Hinduism is God-realization. Hinduism assures that both householders and monks can realize God if they sincerely follow their own spiritual ideal. Many of the spiritually-illumined sages of ancient India such as Ashvapati and King Janaka were family men.

Hinduism offers two major spiritual paths or sets of religious duties—one for householders and the other for monks. The path for householders is called Pravritti Mārga or "the path of permitted sensual desires." The path for monks is Nivritti Mārga or "the path of renunciation of sensual desires."

PRAVRITTI MĀRGA—THE PATH OF PERMITTED SENSUAL DESIRES

According to the *Mahānirvāna-Tantra*[1] the following are the duties of a householder. They fall under the category of Pravritti Mārga.

---

1. See Swāmī Vivekānanda's English translation of the *Mahānirvāna Tantra* in his book *Karma-Yoga*.

The goal of a householder is to realize God. To achieve this goal he should perform all his duties as enjoined by the scriptures. He should constantly work by surrendering the fruits of his actions to God. He should earn a living through honest means and remember that his life is meant for the service of God and the poor and helpless. He should always try to please his parents, looking upon them as tangible representatives of God. In the presence of his parents a householder must not joke, be frivolous, or show anger. If his parents come when he is sitting, he must rise as a mark of respect and honor. He may resume his seat only when asked by his parents to do so.

A householder must not eat before providing food for his parents, his wife and children, and the poor. He should undergo a thousand troubles in order to serve his parents because he must not forget that he owes his body to them.

He must never scold, hurt the feelings of his wife, or show anger towards her. He must always take care of her as if she were his own mother.[2] He must maintain complete fidelity to his wife. He will go to the darkest hell if he craves even mentally for another woman. He must always please his wife with money, clothes, love, faithfulness, and sweet words, and never do anything to hurt her. A man who has succeeded in getting the love of his chaste wife has indeed got the blessings of his religion and acquired all virtues.

---

2. In Hindu society, grown-up sons, even though married, live with their parents and are expected to take care of them. According to the *Taittirīya Upanishad* a son has to serve his mother, looking upon her as a goddess.

A householder must never use improper language in the presence of women nor should he brag about his achievements. He must not say, "I have done this, and I have done that." He must not talk in public of his own fame, nor should he brag about his wealth, power or position. He must not talk about his poverty either. Neither must he divulge to others what someone has confided in him.

He must not give excessive attention to food, clothes or his external appearance. He should maintain the cleanliness of his body, and his heart should be pure. He should always be enthusiastic and active. He must be brave and should fight to resist his enemies like a hero. He must not act like a coward and try to rationalize his cowardice by talking about non-resistance or non-violence. To his friends and relatives, however, he will be as gentle as a lamb.

These will be his duties, in regard to his children:

He should lovingly bring up his son until he is four. Then the son should be properly educated until he is sixteen. When the son is twenty he should be employed in some work and be treated by his father as his equal. His daughter should also be treated and educated the same way. At the time of her marriage her father should give her jewelry and money.

The householder should also take care of his brothers and sisters and their children if they are poor. He has similar duties toward his other relatives, friends and servants, and the people of his own village. If a householder be rich and yet does not help his needy relatives and the poor, he is considered a brute and not a human being.

A householder must never show respect to the wicked nor condone wickedness. He must respect those who are good and endowed with noble qualities. He should enter into friendship with only those who are reliable. Before befriending them he should carefully judge them by their dealings with other people.

He must make sincere and honest efforts to acquire a good name. He must speak the truth. His words should be pleasant and beneficial to others. He must not gamble, and must not be the cause of trouble to others.

A householder who does not struggle to become wealthy through honest means is failing in his moral duty. If he is lazy and leads an idle life, he should be considered immoral. He must be enthusiastic in earning money in order to help others who depend on him.

A householder should engage in social service for the benefit of people. He should excavate reservoirs to provide water for drinking and irrigation, plant shade-trees by the roadside for pedestrians, build shelters for travelers, and construct roads and bridges. Such selfless actions will help the householder to attain the same spiritual goal as the greatest Yogi.[3]

NIVRITTI MĀRGA—THE PATH OF RENUNCIATION OF SENSUAL DESIRES

The path for all-renouncing monks, *Nivritti Mārga*, is quite different from that of the householders. A monk, avowed to celibacy, should be physically and mentally pure. He should respect every woman, looking upon her

---

3. See page 33 for more on the second stage of Aryan life.

as his own mother. Following the ancient tradition, he should maintain his body by begging food from house-holders, lead a life of simplicity, and spend most of his time in the contemplation of God and study of the scriptures. He should not own any home, wealth or property. He should live in a hut, a temple, or under a tree. He must be truthful, nonviolent, serene of mind, and full of compassion for all beings. He should never go to see a king or such dignitaries. If they want they can come and see him, and he should treat them with the same kindness with which he must treat everyone. He should give the same good behavior to all, whether poor or rich, good or wicked. He must be indifferent to praise, blame, pleasure or pain. His only goal in life should be the realization of God.[4]

---

4. See page 36 for more on the fourth stage of Aryan life.

XV

THE FOUR YOGAS

INTRODUCTION

In addition to the Pravritti Mārga and Nivritti Mārga discussed in the previous chapter, Hinduism speaks of many different methods or paths to reach God. Of them four are considered major paths: (1) *Bhakti Yoga*—the path of devotion, (2) *Jnāna Yoga*—the path of rational inquiry, (3) *Rāja Yoga*—the path of mental concentration, and (4) *Karma Yoga*—the path of right action. The Sanskrit word *yoga* means yoke—the "connecting link" between the spiritual aspirant and God. Yoga also means a method or technique to establish mental communion with God.

According to Hinduism all people can be put into four broad categories: (1) the emotional person, (2) the rational person, (3) the meditative person and (4) the habitually overactive person. Bhakti Yoga is suitable for the emotional person. Jnāna Yoga is meant for the rational person. Rāja Yoga is suitable for the meditative person. Karma Yoga is prescribed for the person naturally inclined toward activity.

BHAKTI YOGA—THE PATH OF DEVOTION

This path enables the emotional person to have a direct vision of Personal God or Īshvara. The emotion love,

115

which is abundantly available in everyone, is skillfully used as a means to attain God-vision. Love in human beings is usually present as "selfish love." If selfish love can somehow be sublimated and directed towards God, it becomes an effective means of God-realization. Hindu history and legends tell us about many such instances.

In his youth Tulsīdās, a famous Hindu saint of India, was passionately attached to his young wife. He loved her with all his heart and soul and could not stay away from her even for a single day. His wife had not seen her parents for a while and was eager to visit them, but Tulsīdās would not allow her to go.

One day, however, when Tulsīdās left his village on some errand, his wife went to her parents' home in a nearby village without informing her husband. Tulsīdās came to know this as soon as he returned home and immediately went to his in-laws' home to find his wife. She felt extremely embarrassed at this,[1] and said to her husband, "Shame on you! You can't stay away from me even for a day! Had you been as attached to God as you are to me, perhaps you would have seen Him." This admonition hurt the feelings of Tulsīdās so much that he immediately left his wife and never returned home. He became a monk and a passionate lover of God. In course

---

1. In orthodox Hindu society, direct or indirect display of love or feeling of endearment between a husband and wife in the presence of other people, including close relatives, is considered to be in very poor taste. Such love is expected to be displayed only in the privacy of one's home. Tulsīdās's unexpected arrival at his in-laws' home without an invitation made his sensual attachment to his wife too obvious to her parents. Therefore, she felt extremely embarrassed at her husband's behavior and spoke harshly to Tulsīdās.

of time he was blessed with God-vision and became a saint.

Tulsīdās's life is a beautiful example of how selfish and passionate love can be sublimated and transformed into a means of God-realization. This technique of transforming worldly love into divine love is called Bhakti Yoga.

Bhakti Yoga disciplines consist of maintaining physical and mental purity (*shaucha*), prayer (*prārthanā*), chanting of God's holy name (*japa*), the singing of devotional songs (*gīta*), and the adoration and worship of God (*pūjā* or *upāsanā*).

Worship is of two kinds: (1) external ritualistic worship and (2) mental worship. Mental worship is a kind of meditation and is considered superior to ritualistic worship. It is more suitable for those who have made adequate progress in spiritual life. Ritualistic worship is suitable for beginners. In ritualistic worship, images or holy symbols are used.[2]

Chanting the holy name of God, or *japa*, is done in several ways. When it is done audibly by pronouncing the holy name correctly, it is called *vāchika japa*. When the chanting is done by moving the tongue and the lips in such a manner that it can be heard only by the chanter and no one else, it is called *upāmshu japa*. In the third type of chanting the Holy Name is repeated mentally without moving the tongue or the lips. This type of silent chanting is called *mānasa japa*. Among these the third one is considered superior to the second, and the second superior to the first.

---

2. For a detailed description of ritualistic worship please see the next chapter.

Encouragement is given to develop special mental attitudes that generate a feeling of closeness to God. The attitudes are *shānta* or a serene and dispassionate attitude, *dāsya* or the attitude of a servant, *sakhya* or the attitude of a friend, *vātsalya* or the attitude of a mother towards her child, and *madhura* or the sweet attitude of a loving wife towards her husband. Any of these attitudes helps spiritual aspirants develop a feeling of closeness to God. These five different spiritual attitudes differ from one another in the quality and intensity of love associated with them.

In the serene or shānta attitude, the intensity of love is relatively less pronounced. The devotee does not want any personal relationship with God and yet wants to know Him with one-pointed yearning of heart.

In the dāsya or serving attitude, the devotee looks upon himself as the servant of God and through his loving service wants to please Him. As a servant, however, he naturally has to maintain some distance between himself and God.

In the sakhya or friendly attitude, the relationship between the devotee and God is much closer. The devotee loves God by looking upon Him as his dearest friend, and at the same time expects reciprocal love from God.

In the vātsalya or motherly attitude, the devotee looks upon God as his child, and like a mother showers all his love and affection on Him. The devotee does not expect anything in return from God.

In the madhura or sweet attitude, the devotee loves God with the same intensity of love that a faithful and loving wife has for her husband. The reader should understand very clearly that in this attitude the devotee is not even aware of his or her body or sex. This is entirely a spiritual relationship.

Other than these attitudes, the devotee can also look upon God as his father or mother and himself as the child. Many great saints of Bengal, such as Rāmprasād, Kamalākānta, and Shrī Rāmakrishna, maintained this attitude and looked upon God as the Divine Mother.

With the help of these spiritual attitudes, and following the other disciplines of Bhakti Yoga, the devotee's love for God becomes more and more mature. This love gradually purifies his mind and enables him to have the vision of the Personal God or Īshvara.

JNĀNA YOGA—THE PATH OF RATIONAL INQUIRY

According to one American author, a theologian who belongs to the Episcopal Church, "The top 10% of the people who are most creative, constructive and thoughtful, do not have much to do with churches. To them the canons of reason come first, making faith secondary and questionable."[3] It is these people who can especially benefit from Jnāna Yoga. Such a person may say, "I can't accept things on faith alone. I have difficulty believing in what the saints or the prophets say. How can I be sure that they are not self-deluded or mistaken? I can't believe in God because I have not experienced or known Him yet. Besides, I am not even sure if this world really exists; the whole thing may be just an illusion or my mental projection!"

---

3. Dr. Joseph Fletcher, *Seattle Post-Intelligencer*, 2 November 1974, sec. A, p. 10.

Jnāna Yoga will try to resolve these doubts by saying, "You doubt the existence of this world and also the experiences of the saints and prophets. Your reasoning may disprove the existence of all this, but you can't disprove your own existence as the doubter. Therefore, as a doubter you must exist. But who are you 'really'? Are you your physical body, vital energy, senses, or mind? You can't deny that you have the awareness that you own them. The 'owner' and the 'owned' can't be the same. They have to be different from each other. Therefore, you are not your physical body, energy, senses or mind; you are different from them all. Try to know your true identity; try to know who you really are."

The first instruction of Jnāna Yoga is *"Ātmānam viddhi"* or "Know thyself." This instruction is based on the fundamental teaching of the Vedas that everything in this universe is divine.[4] As divinity is present everywhere, it must also be present in all human beings. The true Self of man or the indwelling Spirit is this divinity which forms the very core of one's being or existence. This true Self is not the ego. According to Hinduism, the ego or "I-ness" is purely mental; it is an idea only. The true Self of man or the indwelling Spirit is different from this ego. The goal of students of Jnāna Yoga is to gain 100% conviction that this true Self is divine.

First a student has to go through some preparatory disciplines, such as the observance of moral and ethical practices in order to strengthen the will or mental muscles. Then he has to purify his mind through selfless work. Once the student's mind has been purified, the

---

4. *Sarvam khalv idam Brahma*—"All, indeed, is God."

spiritual teacher asks the student to meditate on the divinity of his true inner Self.[5]

In order to follow the instructions of his teacher the student has to go through three steps: (1) *Shravana*, (2) *Manana* and (3) *Nididhyāsana*. *Shravana* means "hearing." The student has to hear from the mouth of his teacher the ultimate truth about himself. The teacher says to his student, *"Tat tvam asi,"* which means, "You are that Divine Reality" or "You are God."

The student must have implicit faith (*shraddhā*) in the words of his teacher. The purity of mind which the student has acquired through his preliminary spiritual practice enables him to have such faith. Consequently he says to himself, "My teacher has said that I am divine. But my experience is that I am still a mortal, limited in my power and knowledge. I don't feel that I am eternal, all-knowing, all-powerful and all-pervading. How can I then be divine? But my teacher's words can't be false. There must be something in me which is divine. Let me try to find it. Obviously my body is not divine, because it is transient and subject to decay and death. My vital energy can't be divine either, because it is limited and not infinite. For the same reason my senses and mind can't be divine."

Through such mentation or *manana* the student tries to negate everything that is not Divine in himself; this negation is called the process of *neti* (lit. "not this") in Sanskrit. Gradually his contemplation on his divine Self becomes one-pointed. This is called *nididhyāsana,* and it eventually leads him to the divine core of his being.

5. According to Jnāna Yoga, *upāsanā* or worship of God can also purify the mind.

At that stage he no longer is conscious of his physical body or the external world. His mind and ego have, as it were, melted away in the infinite ocean of divinity. The mind is then said to be in nirvikalpa samādhi. Through such samādhi he comes to experience his identity with the Impersonal God or Nirguna Brahman. Knowing one's divine identity or divine Self is the ultimate goal of Jnāna Yoga. This divine identity is the ultimate Truth which a student of Jnāna Yoga experiences through nirvikalpa samādhi at the end of his spiritual quest.

There is, however, a lower state of samādhi, called savikalpa samādhi, where the ego of the meditator is still retained in a very subdued form.

RĀJA YOGA—THE PATH OF MENTAL CONCENTRATION

Eight steps of Rāja Yoga

Rāja Yoga is most suitable for a person with a natural tendency to explore and know his own mind in order to gain total mastery over it. The founder of this yoga is the renowned sage Patanjali. Rāja Yoga is ordinarily called *Yoga*; it is also called *Kriyā Yoga*. The disciplines of Rāja Yoga consist of eight steps: (1) *yama* or inner restraint, (2) *niyama* or cultivating good habits, (3) *āsana* or posture, (4) *prānāyāma* or the art of controlling the breath, (5) *pratyāhāra* or withdrawal of the senses, (6) *dhāranā* or fixing the mind on a chosen object, (7) *dhyāna* or meditation, and (8) *samādhi* or intense mental concentration.

Yama or inner restraint consists in abstention from violence, falsehood, stealing, indulging in passions or carnal desires, and accepting unnecessary gifts from other people.

Niyama consists in the cultivation of good habits, such as keeping the body and mind clean, contentment, austerity, regularity in the study of religious books, and submission to God.

Āsana means sitting postures suitable for prolonged contemplation or meditation. Rāja Yoga prescribes various postures for that purpose.

Prānāyāma, or breath control, is a type of rhythmic breathing which helps in calming down and concentrating a restless mind. It consists in inhalation, retention of breath, and exhalation, all done according to techniques which can be learned only from expert teachers of Rāja Yoga. Prānāyāma, if not practiced under the guidance of a capable teacher, can do irreparable physical and mental damage to one who engages in it.

Pratyāhāra is the art of withdrawing the senses and the mind from external objects.

Dhāranā is the art of fixing the mind on a chosen object of contemplation for a short period of time.

Dhyāna or meditation is a more mature state of dhāranā. When the mind is concentrated on the object of contemplation without any break or disturbance for a longer period of time, it is called dhyāna. In both dhāranā and dhyāna the meditator's mind retains its distinction from the object of meditation. Dhyāna at a higher state of maturity is called *samādhi.*

Samādhi is a state of the most intense mental concentration on the object of contemplation. The meditator can have different types of samādhi, one superior to the other, because of the various levels of mental concentration.

A relatively inferior samādhi is called *samprajnāta samādhi*. The power of controlling nature comes to a person who attains this samādhi. In this samādhi the meditator still retains his ego.

In the highest type of samādhi, called *asamprajnāta samādhi*, the ego disappears completely. In this state of intense concentration the mind loses itself or melts away in the object of its contemplation. It is no longer aware of its own independent existence. In other words, the mind is without thought. This samādhi is the goal of Rāja Yoga.

According to Rāja Yoga, the uncontrolled and impure mind of a person can be compared to a lake with many waves and ripples in it. Its water is not clear because it has many impurities. At the bottom of the lake there is a powerful light. In this particular analogy the waves are the thoughts, the turbidity of water is the impurity of the mind, and the light source at the bottom of the lake is the soul or inner Divine Self of the person.

The light of the inner Self is not visible on the surface because of the cloudy water and numerous waves in the lake. If the lake can be made free from waves, and its water freed from impurities, the light at the bottom will shine forth. In other words, the Divine Self of the person will manifest itself in all its glory when the person's mind becomes pure and free of all thoughts. The goal of Rāja Yoga is to create such a state of mind. This state of mind is asamprajnāta samādhi. Anyone who has been able to attain this samādhi has attained the highest level of saintliness.

Past mental impressions & how to free the mind from them

The impurity of the mind is primarily caused by the accumulated thoughts of the past. According to Rāja Yoga, not a single thought is ever lost. Every thought eventually goes down to the subconscious level and remains there as an impression. There are innumerable impressions of past thoughts in the subconscious level of an average mind. These impressions are called *samskāras*[6] in Sanskrit. The techniques of Rāja Yoga, such as meditation or dhyāna, can help cleanse the mind of these samskāras.

An analogy will make this idea clear. Let us suppose a person is standing on the shore of a lake with a roll of absorbent paper towels. He starts throwing the paper towels one by one into the lake. The towels first float on the surface for a few minutes and then sink and settle at the bottom of the lake, layer by layer, one on top of the other.

The lake is the mind and the paper towels are the thoughts. The paper towels when floating are thoughts at the conscious level of mind. In their submerged state at the bottom of the lake, they are samskāras or impressions of past thoughts in the subconscious level of mind. These impressions are like so many negatives of photographs. They have the ability to produce picture prints under favorable circumstances. Similarly, the samskāras have the potential to become conscious thoughts again if a suitable mental environment is created for them.

---

6. The word *samskāra* in this context does not mean "sacrament."

Meditation is contemplation done with great mental concentration. When a person meditates, his concentrated thought, like a laser beam, penetrates through the inner layers of his mind and arrives at the bottom where the samskāras are. The concentrated thought, like an underwater probe, starts disturbing the accumulated samskāras. As a result, they gradually get dislodged and rise one by one to the conscious level. They become conscious thoughts again. The meditator should watch the rejuvenated thoughts like a disinterested observer and must not act upon them. The old thoughts, once they have risen to the conscious level, burst like so many air bubbles and disappear. This is how, through the practice of meditation, one can purify one's mind by gradually getting rid of old impressions or samskāras. If, however, the meditator acts upon those rejuvenated thoughts, he will create new samskāras and his mind will not be cleansed.

Siddhis or supernatural powers

In the course of practicing Rāja Yoga, as a student gains considerable mastery over his mind, he acquires eight extraordinary powers called *ashtasiddhi*: (1) *animā*—the capacity to grow as small as a molecule and penetrate solid objects, (2) *laghimā*—extreme lightness of body or the ability to levitate, (3) *vyāpti*—the ability to expand, (4) *prākāmya*—the acquisition of irresistible will, (5) *mahimā*—the ability to make the body extremely large, (6) *īshitva*—acquiring godlike powers, (7) *vashitva*—the power to bring everything under one's control, and (8) *kāmāvasāyitā*—the ability to obtain whatever one desires.

Other powers may also come: the ability to fly (*khe-chari-vidyā*), the conquest of death (*mrityunjaya-vidyā*), the ability to acquire hidden treasure (*pātāla-siddhi*), the ability to enter another's body (*kāya-siddhi*), knowledge of the past, present, and future (*trikāla-jnāna*), the power to die at will (*ichchhā-mrityu*), the power to make oneself invisible (*antardhāna*), going beyond hunger and thirst (*kshutpipāsā-nivritti*), and the power to understand all animal languages (*sarvabhūtaruta-jnāna*).

The student is advised not to use any of these powers (*siddhis*). These powers are like milestones on the path of spiritual progress, but can be obstacles to reaching the ultimate spiritual goal. If the student stops at any of these milestones, trapped by the lure of these powers, he cannot reach the goal. He should ignore them and proceed steadfastly along his spiritual path until the goal is reached. Once he reaches the goal, his inherent divinity will manifest itself in all its splendor and he will be free from all human limitations. He will become a saint.

Kundalinī power & the six chakras

According to Rāja Yoga, the spiritual power in man usually lies in a dormant state. Like a coiled-up snake in a state of hybernation, this power usually remains asleep near the lower extremity of a person's backbone. A coil is called *kundala* in Sanskrit. Kundalinī means something which is coiled up, such as a snake. Rāja Yoga helps one to awaken this dormant spiritual power called kundalinī through meditation and other spiritual practices.

The human backbone or spinal column is like so many 8's piled one on top of the other, forming two vertical channels side by side. The vital energy or nerve current of a person works in his body by passing through these two channels. The left channel is called *idā* and the right

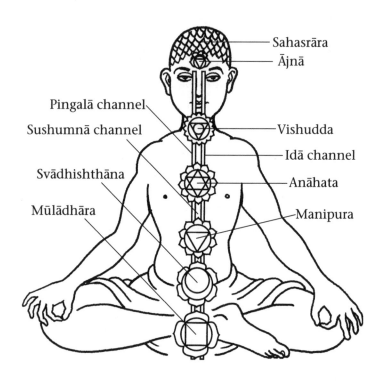

Sahasrāra
Ājnā
Pingalā channel
Sushumnā channel
Vishudda
Idā channel
Svādhishthāna
Anāhata
Mūlādhāra
Manipura

The Chakras

channel *pingalā*. If a person's breath is stronger through his left nostril when he exhales, it is an indication that his vital energy is flowing through the idā channel at that time. Similarly, if the breath is stronger through his right nostril, then the energy is flowing through the pingalā channel. When a person does a copious amount of physical activity, his energy usually flows through the pingalā channel. When resting, his energy flows through the idā channel.

There is a third channel inside the backbone which is between the idā and pingalā. Its name is *sushumnā*. Normally the sushumnā channel remains closed. It opens up when the kundalinī power is awakened. The awakened kundalinī power starts coursing through the sushumnā channel towards the brain. When that happens, the spiritual aspirant enters into an altogether different domain of experience. He starts having genuine spiritual experiences. The awakened kundalinī power, as it starts moving toward the brain, seems to pass through different doors, each one of which introduces the spiritual aspirant to a newer set of genuine spiritual experiences. Each of these doors or levels of spiritual experience is called a *chakra*. Rāja Yoga speaks of seven such levels, the topmost one of which is *sahasrāra*. The sahasrāra is located somewhere inside the brain. The lowest one, which is at the lower end of the spinal cord, is called *mūlādhāra*. The next higher chakra is *svādhishthāna*, then in succession come *manipura*, *anāhata*, *vishuddha*, *ājnā*, and *sahasrāra*.

In Hinduism we read about three types of space. The space in which we and the stars and planets are posited is called *mahākāsha* or "outer space." Our dream world or the objects of our imagination exist in *chittākāsha* or mental space. All genuine spiritual experiences take place in *chidākāsha* or "knowledge space." A person gets access to chidākāsha only when his kundalinī power has awakened and entered into the sushumnā channel. All experiences in the chittākāsha are no other than imagination or hallucination compared to the genuine spiritual experiences in the chidākāsha. When the kundalinī power reaches the sahasrāra through the sushumnā channel, the spiritual aspirant becomes spiritually illumined. He reaches the goal of Yoga—he attains asamprajnāta samādhi.

Although Rāja Yoga literally means the "King of all Yogas," there is some hazard connected with its practice. In the words of Swāmī Vivekānanda, a past master of Rāja Yoga, "There must be perfect chastity, in thought, word and deed; without it the practice of Rāja Yoga is dangerous, and may lead to insanity." Aspirants who want to practice this yoga are advised to heed these words of caution.

KARMA YOGA—THE PATH OF RIGHT ACTION

In the context of Karma Yoga the Sanskrit word *karma* means work or action. Thinking also may be considered karma. A verse of the *Bhagavad Gītā* says, "No one can ever stay without doing work even for a moment."[7] Work, which can be both physical and mental, is inevitable. Therefore, the impact of work on the life of the doer can never be overemphasized. Even the attempt not to work turns out to be work. The following story will clearly explain this idea.

---

7. *Bhagavad Gītā* 3/5.

During his wanderings in India a holy man came to a village. He stayed there for a few days and impressed the villagers greatly with one of his yogic powers. He displayed the extraordinary ability to kill or revive anything by sprinkling water on it while chanting mystic words or *mantras*.

During the holy man's stay in the village, a young boy served him daily by doing various chores. As a result, the holy man grew very fond of the boy. He called the boy aside one morning and said, "I am leaving this afternoon, but before I leave I would like to give you a gift. I have had this rosary for many years; I give it to you. You may use it when you say your daily prayers." But the boy said, "Sir, if you don't mind, I would rather have some other gift from you." The holy man said, "I am a man of very few possessions. What else can I give you?" The boy said, "Please teach me how to give or take life as you do. I want this gift from you."

The holy man, bound by his commitment, had to teach the boy the mantras and said, "My child, before you chant them you have to be very careful about one thing. You must never think of a black cat. If you do, the mantras won't work." "I'll never do that," the boy assured him, and taking leave of the holy man immediately went towards his neighborhood.

Reaching his neighborhood, he called all his young friends and said, "I've the power to kill or bring anything back to life. The holy man has taught me how to do it!" But his friends would not believe him. So, the boy decided to display his power.

He had a pet cat. After tying the cat to a post he sprinkled water on it and chanted the mantras. But nothing happened; the cat did not even faint—what to speak of dying! The boy became a laughingstock in his neighborhood. He ran to the holy man and said, "Sir, the mantras didn't work. I feel very humiliated." The holy man said, "Did you heed my warning? Did you, by any chance, think of a black cat when you chanted those words?" The boy said, "Sir, I may be young, but I'm not stupid. When I was chanting those words I kept telling myself all the time that I mustn't think of a black cat." The holy man said, "That's as good as thinking of a black cat. In trying not to think of a black cat you actually thought of one! That's why the mantras didn't work."

According to Hinduism, work, which is inevitable, has one great disadvantage. Any work done with attachment to its fruits generates a kind of psychological bondage for the doer. Consider a florist who with great care has been trying to grow for the first time an extremely rare and delicate variety of rose in his garden. When the roses are about to bloom, he gets a call from a close friend who says, "I am going on a trip to Europe for a month. I shall be very happy if you come with me. All expenses are mine, you don't have to worry about anything!" But the florist, even though he would like to go on that trip, feels that he cannot do so. It is as though his attachment to his exotic roses has put him in some kind of bondage. If he could shake off his attachment to the roses, he instantly would be free from this bondage and could go anywhere he liked.

So also with every action that a person does. An action done with attachment to its fruits puts the doer in bondage. Karma Yoga teaches the secret of how to maintain one's freedom even though working all the time.

The secret consists in working without any attachment to the fruits of the work. Attachment is selfish involvement, and always rooted in selfish expectations. Therefore, work done without attachment to its fruits is no other than work done unselfishly.

The art and science of performing unselfish work is Karma Yoga or the Yoga of Right Action. It is not easy to work unselfishly. A student of Karma Yoga is often instructed to work for the pleasure of God. If work is done for God, and not for one's own sake, then that work becomes unselfish work.

It may be argued, however, that even when a person works for the sake of God, the desire for his own spiritual progress actually motivates his action. Therefore, such action cannot be called truly unselfish action. But according to Karma Yoga the desire for one's own spiritual progress is not considered selfishness; it is considered "enlightened" selfishness. It is not harmful.

The saint Shrī Rāmakrishna makes this point clear with the help of an analogy. He says that uneducated villagers in rural Bengal[8] believe that sweets and candies are harmful for a person suffering from an acid stomach. According to them, sweets and candies aggravate acidity. But they believe that rock candy—which itself is a candy—is an antidote for acidity. Similarly, the desire for one's own spiritual progress, even though a selfish one, is an antidote for selfishness. It is conducive to one's ultimate spiritual enlightenment.

---

8. Bengal is a state in India.

Work done for the sake of God gradually transforms the doer's mind into a purified mind, devoid of the sense of agency or doership. Such a mind alone can enable a person to have God-vision, which is the goal of Karma Yoga.

Karma Yoga also liberates a person from the chain of repeated births and deaths. Every link of this chain is created by the person's own *karmaphala*.[9] If the person can learn to work in such a manner that the fruits of his work do not come back to him, then no new links will be created. As a result, the continuity of the chain of repeated births and deaths will be broken, and he will become free. The secret of gaining this freedom is to work without attachment to its results. If the doer does not want the fruits of his action, the fruits will never come to him.

It is like a person who has deposited one million dollars in a bank with the instruction that the income from his investment must not be credited to his account; it should be given in charity to a church. In this case, the account holder is not expecting the fruits of his investment. The result of his investment—the interest income—will not come back to him. In the same manner, a person who works while disowning the fruits of his action will break a link in the chain of repeated births and deaths and will not be born again. In other words, he will attain liberation.

According to Hinduism, work in itself is neither good nor bad. The mental attitude with which work is done determines if the work is good or bad. A surgeon performs surgery on a patient and the patient dies. Even

---

9. Sanskrit: the fruits of action.

though the patient dies at the hands of the surgeon, the doctor is not considered a criminal because he had a helping attitude toward the patient. He wanted the patient to be cured. In another case, an assassin who has killed someone is considered a criminal, because he had a harmful attitude. He deliberately wanted to harm his victim. The consequences of the action in these two externally similar cases will be diametrically opposite to each other—one good, the other bad.

But merely maintaining the right attitude toward work is not enough in Karma Yoga. The doer must also know how to work properly. Otherwise, he will not have the desired spiritual progress. The following story will make this idea clear.

A soldier had a pet monkey. He trained the monkey to do many intelligent tricks. One hot summer afternoon, the soldier was having a nap lying on the grass in the shade of a large tree. He had put his sword by his side on the grass. The monkey was sitting near the soldier and keeping a close watch over its master. The monkey noticed that a fly kept sitting again and again on the soldier's face and disturbing his sleep. The monkey did not like it. When the fly sat on the soldier's face again the monkey unsheathed its master's sword and with one swift and powerful stroke tried to kill the fly. The fly flew away and the soldier died!

The monkey had the right attitude; it wanted to help its master. But its method was all wrong. Similarly, a person who has the right attitude toward work, but does not know how to work properly, will not have the full benefit of Karma Yoga.

XVI

WORSHIP OF GOD

WORSHIP OF GOD THROUGH IMAGES

There is a notion in the minds of many people that Hindus are idolatrous because they usually use images to worship God. This is not at all correct. Images are no other than various "symbols" of God's (Īshvara's) power and glory. Through such tangible symbols a Hindu tries to establish contact with the intangible Īshvara. Just as a photograph of a person's father is not his real father, but only reminds him of his father, so also an image symbolizing some powers or glories of God is never considered by a Hindu to be God Himself. It only helps him to remember God. The image, which is a symbol, acts like a link between God and His worshiper. When through such adoration and worship the worshiper establishes mental communion with God, worship ends. Then there is no more need for images. That is why Hindus often discard the images after worship and immerse them in either lakes or rivers.

Images are made of various materials, such as clay, stone, wood, pure metal or metal alloys. Usually less expensive clay or wooden images are discarded after worship. Images made of more expensive and durable material are repeatedly used.

The Indo-Aryans used fire as the symbol of God during the Vedic period. Since God is present everywhere, anything existing in the universe can be chosen as His symbol. They chose fire, the dispeller of darkness, the symbol of purity, the giver of warmth, as the symbol of God.

It is in the very nature of true love to want to offer to the beloved what is most dear to the lover. During worship the Vedic Aryans used to offer to God browned butter, oats, sesame seeds, fruits, and other foods they were fond of. After the offering was consumed by fire they had the psychological satisfaction that God had accepted their offering. Yet they were fully aware that God never really needs any food. God, being perfect, is not wanting in anything. They also knew that they could not offer to God anything which did not already belong to Him.

This ancient tradition of worshiping God by using fire as His symbol is still followed by some Hindus, although various other forms of ritualistic worship were later introduced by sages in the post-Vedic period. The highest form of worship, however, is mental worship or meditation, where no external symbols or images are used.

Some images used by Hindus to worship God have several arms, or more than one head. The images also have different colors. To portray God's various powers many arms are used, each arm symbolizing a different power of God. Some images have one hundred, or even one thousand arms, to indicate that God has infinite powers. For the same reason, Hindus sometimes put more than one head on images. The blue color of an image indicates the unfathomable and infinite nature of God. Similarly, other colors may symbolize other aspects of God.

In order to keep the body and mind alert during worship, the worshiper is advised not to worship with a full stomach. Therefore, some worshipers fast until they have finished their worship. But such fasting is not obligatory. Those who are unable to fast can take a light meal such as a small quantity of fruits and milk before worship.

In external ritualistic worship the worshiper uses flowers, water, light, a hand fan and a piece of cloth as symbols of the five elements which, according to Hinduism, constitute this entire universe. Different foods and other kinds of gifts are also offered to God.

The worship starts with purification. Every item used in the worship has to be purified by the thought of the worshiper. Holy words associated with God, called *mantras*, are chanted by the worshiper along with thoughts of purification such as "May the flowers be pure and holy; may the water be pure and holy." In this manner he purifies every item used for worship. Then he purifies every part of his own body. After that he has to think of the divinity present in himself. He prays to God that, by God's grace, his inherent divinity becomes manifest and thus he may become fit to worship God. According to Hinduism, only a person who has been able to manifest his inherent divinity can really appreciate and adore God. The worshiper then offers flowers to God as a symbol of his love and devotion. He offers food and other gifts, and last of all he presents the symbols of the five elements to God as though to make the statement that he cannot offer to God anything that does not already belong to Him. By using those five symbols he offers the entire universe to God. This offering is called *Ārati* or *Ārātrika*. The worshiper also prays to God for the well-being of all the creatures in the world, as well as for his own spiritual illumination. Throughout the course of this worship, the worshiper has the opportunity to constantly think of purity and holiness. As a result, through repeated ritualistic worship he gradually becomes holy; because what one thinks, that one eventually becomes.

Animal sacrifice in ritualistic worship

In some forms of Hindu ritualistic worship, particularly those influenced by the disciplines of Tantra, animal sacrifice is sometimes permitted. Keeping in mind the important scriptural injunction, "Do not commit violence to any being,"[1] one may wonder how the sacrifice of animals, no matter how infrequently, can be allowed by Hinduism.

Not only animals, but all forms of life are sacred to Hinduism. It does not encourage violence towards anything. Hinduism considers every food impure because it is directly or indirectly connected with violence. For instance, food grains such as wheat and rice have life in them. The same is true for other kinds of food, animal or vegetable. Eating them is no other than destroying life or committing violence. Even honey, which seems such an innocent food, is acquired by robbing bees of the fruits of their hard labor. For these reasons, Hindus are expected to offer whatever they eat to God first, either mentally or ritually, in order to purify that food.

According to Hinduism, any food offered to God with love and devotion is sanctified by God. It becomes free

---

1. *Na himsyāt sarvabhūtāni* in Sanskrit. *Mahābhārata* (Shantiparva) 269/5.

from defect or impurity. A Hindu is supposed to eat only sanctified food for his physical and spiritual well-being.

In ancient times most Indo-Aryans ate meat with certain restrictions about which animals could be killed and eaten.[2] Rather than recklessly butchering animals and eating their meat, it was considered better to sacrifice the animal as an offering to God and then eat that sanctified meat. Any meat from animals not offered to God would be treated as inedible.[3] In this manner some restraint was imposed on the wanton killing of animals for human consumption. In addition, animal sacrifice in the presence of God was supposed to be interpreted as killing the animality or lower nature of the worshiper in order to manifest the worshiper's higher nature or inherent divinity.

It should be clearly understood that even though Hinduism sometimes allows animal sacrifice, it never encourages it. Even the scriptures of Tantra allow other symbols, such as a pumpkin, ash gourd, squash or any other fruit, to represent the worshiper's lower nature or animality. Such symbolic fruits can be sacrificed instead of animals in the presence of God.

In today's India, animal sacrifice is very rare. The vast majority of the Hindus are vegetarians and they do not want animals to be killed for any reason. The small number of Hindus who eat meat buy it from butcher shops as is done in the West.

---

2. *The Laws of Manu*, V/18, 22-23.
3. The term in Sanskrit is *vritha mānsa*.

HINDU RELIGIOUS FESTIVALS

There are numerous major and minor festivals in Hinduism.[4] The same religious festivals are not observed in all parts of India. Deepāvali, or Diwālī, and Mahāshivarātri are two major festivals observed all over India. Deepāvalī is also called "the festival of lights." Holi or Dol Pūrnimā is another important festival observed during the advent of spring all over northern and eastern India. In eastern India, particularly in Bengal, Durgā Pūjā, Kālī Pūjā and Sarasvatī Pūjā are the most important festivals. Durgā Pūjā lasts for four days. In the northeastern part of India, particularly in the state of Assam, Bahāg Bihu, Kāti Bihu and Māgh Bihu are the major festivals. Ganesh Pūjā or Ganesh Chaturthī is a major festival in western India. In southern India Deepāvalī, Navarātri and Pongal are the important festivals. Navarātri lasts for nine days. Northern and central India also observe Navarātri as a major festival.

In Nepal one of the major Hindu festivals is Bhrātri Dvitīyā, or Brother's Day. This festival, also known as Bhāi Duj, is also very popular all over northern and eastern India. In addition to these festivals, Janmāshtamī, Rām Navamī, Rakshā Bandhan, Ratha Yātrā, Chhat Parab, Vaishākhī and the birth anniversaries of various saints are observed in different parts of India.

The minor festivals are too numerous to mention. Every county in India has its own special minor worships or festivals. During some of the major festivals, such as Deepāvalī, Navarātri, Durgā Pūjā and Bhrātri Dvitīyā, gifts are exchanged as is done during Christmas in western countries.

---

4. See "Appendix B" on page 195 for a list of the major Hindu religious festivals.

144   THE ESSENTIALS OF HINDUISM

XVII

MANTRAS AND SACRED SYMBOLS

INTRODUCTION

During a religious discourse, a Hindu saint told the assembled group that a person who chants a *mantra* (the holy name of God) regularly for many years, develops a pure mind which enables him to see God. At this, someone in the audience stood up and said, "Sir, I can't believe in the efficacy of mantras. A mantra is just a word. How can it have the power to purify anyone's mind and give him God-vision?" "What! You don't believe in the power of mantras?" exclaimed the saint, "You're the worst fool I've ever seen in my whole life!"

Since the saint had called him a fool in the presence of the entire audience, the man felt extremely humiliated. His face reddened and he started shaking with suppressed anger. Pointing out his reaction, the saint said, "You don't believe in the power of words, but look at the power of the word 'fool'—what a strong effect it's had on you! And yet you deny the power of mantras?"

In Hinduism, a mantra is not like any other word; it is special. Its association with God makes it sacred and spiritually beneficial. By chanting a mantra repeatedly with love and devotion a person can become spiritually illumined. The derivative meaning of the word mantra is "something by reflecting on which a person is saved (from danger or the bondage of this world)."

In India, spiritual aspirants want to receive mantras from saints or holy men. Such mantras are considered far more effective than mantras picked from a book. The following hypothetical case will explain why.

Let us suppose a patient has gone to his doctor for a checkup. The doctor detects some malignancy in the patient's body. As a result, the patient becomes very worried and upset. Then he returns home and gives the bad news to his wife. Seeing him extremely upset, his wife says to him, "Darling, don't be upset. It's lucky your cancer has been detected so early; you'll be cured." Her words, however, cannot relieve her husband of his worry and anxiety.

A few days later the patient goes to see the best cancer specialist in town. The specialist examines him carefully and says, "You're indeed lucky, the type of cancer you have can be completely cured." Like magic the specialist's words instantly relieve the patient's anxiety.

Both the specialist and the patient's wife have said that he would be cured, but the specialist's words have far more telling effect. His medical training and years of experience in treating cancer have made his words more convincing and effective.

In the same way, a mantra given by a spiritually illumined teacher has his entire life's spiritual experience behind the mantra. A mantra picked by a student from a holy book will undoubtedly help, but not nearly as effectively as a mantra obtained from an illumined teacher.

In addition, a mantra which already has helped someone to have God-realization acquires great spiritual potency. Such a mantra is called a *siddha mantra*. A siddha mantra, if given by a teacher to a student, is more effective than others.

THE SACRED SYMBOL *OM*

Among the sacred mantras or holy words of Hinduism, the monosyllabic word *Om* is the most ancient and undoubtedly the most important. This holy syllable, which signifies God, has been frequently mentioned in the Vedas and other scriptures of Hinduism. The syllable Om can also be spelled as AUM. It is also called *Pranava*. Each of the three letters A, U and M has a special meaning. According to one interpretation, "A" stands for creation, "U" stands for preservation, and "M" indicates destruction or dissolution. As God in Hinduism is the creator, preserver and destroyer of this universe, Om or Aum is a suitable name of God. According to another interpretation, the three letters forming AUM indicate the three lokas (planes of existence) of this universe—both gross and subtle—*Svarga* (heaven), *Martya* (earth) and *Pātāla*

Om or Aum

(netherworld). As the omnipresent God is immanent in these three lokas, Aum is considered a symbol of God.

Aum is also a sonic or auditory symbol of God. All the words produced by the human vocal organ can be represented by Aum. The vocal organ of a person starts with the throat and ends with the lips. "A" is produced in the back of the throat, "U" in the center of the mouth, and "M" by the lips. Therefore, AUM is a symbol of all the words which the vocal organ can produce. Then again, all that exists in this universe can be represented by words, and all words are produced by the vocal organ. Thus the entire universe can be represented by Aum. As God covers the entire universe with His presence, Aum symbolizes God.

Aum is a non-personal as well as a nondenominational symbol. It can, therefore, be used by Hindus of all sects and denominations. Just like the cross in Christianity or the menorah in Judaism, the pictorial image of Aum is used as a symbol of Hinduism.

THE GĀYATRĪ MANTRA

The *Gāyatrī Mantra* is also known as the *Sāvitrī Mantra*. It is one of the most important mantras in the Hindu scriptures. It is found in the *Rig-Veda*.[1] The mantra is in the form of a prayer: "Aum, we meditate on the effulgence of that Adorable Divine Being, who is the source and projector of the three worlds—the earthly plane (*Bhūrloka*), the subtle ethereal plane (*Bhuvarloka*), and the heavenly plane (*Svarloka*). May that Supreme Divine Being stimulate our intelligence in order that we may realize the Supreme Truth."[2] This mantra is recited daily

---

1. *Rig-Veda* III/62/10.

by Hindus of the three upper castes after they have been invested with the sacred thread (*Upavīta*).

Each Vedic mantra is addressed to a deity. Also, each Vedic mantra is associated with the name of the sage to whom the mantra was first revealed. Every Vedic mantra, like a verse, has a meter. The Sāvitrī Mantra (revealed to the Sage Vishwāmitra) is composed in the meter Gāyatrī, this is why its other name is Gāyatrī Mantra.

MANTRAS AND YANTRAS IN THE DISCIPLINE OF TANTRA

Mantras are very important in the discipline of Tantra. Any mantra of the Tantra tradition, among other things, has two important ingredients: (1) the *vīja* (seed) and (2) *shakti* (power). The vīja is a monosyllabic word endowed with great spiritual potency. The vīja is also called a *vīja-mantra*. There can be many vīja-mantras[3] suitable for different deities. Every mantra of the Tantra tradition starts with a vīja-mantra. The Tantra system claims that a mantra accompanied by a vīja has great spiritual potency. Repetition of such a mantra received from a guru enhances the prospect of God-vision. It is also believed that whenever any offering is given to a deity by chanting such a mantra, the deity immediately accepts that offering.[4]

---

2. In Sanskrit: "*Aum bhūr-bhuvah-svah-tat-savitur-varenyam-bhargo devasya dhīmahi dhiyo yo nah prachodayāt.*" For more details about Gāyatrī Mantra please read Swāmī Mukhyānanda, *Om, Gāyatrī and Sandhyā* (Mylapore, Madras, India: Sri Ramakrishna Math, 1989).
3. Examples of vīja-mantras are *hrīng, klīng, shlīng,* etc.
4. Swāmī Swāhānanda, *Meditation and Other Spiritual Disciplines* (Calcutta, India: Advaita Ashrama, 1983), 14.

Yantras are mystic holy diagrams associated with the worship rituals of Tantra. Some yantras are used as symbols of God in the Tāntrika[5] worship.

Yantra of the Divine Mother

---

5. *Tāntrika* is an adjective derived from the word Tantra.

XVIII

TEMPLES

INTRODUCTION

During the Vedic period, God was worshiped by the Hindus using fire as His symbol. Under the open sky, they would erect a platform, light a holy fire on it, and offer oblations into the fire. They did not need temples for their worship.

Scholars are not exactly sure when the Indo-Aryans first started using temples. It is very likely that the first temples were made of mud or wood. For obvious reasons, temples made out of these materials did not survive long. Later, more durable materials such as brick and stone were used to build the temples. Studying the ancient temples, scholars have concluded that some of them were probably built around the first century A.D., if not earlier.

TEMPLE SITES

Hindu temples are usually built in places of great scenic beauty: on river banks, in the hills, on the shores of lakes or by the sea. There are also beautiful cave temples carved out of cliffs.

TEMPLE ARCHITECTURE

The architecture of Hindu temples is varied, but they have in common: (1) a dome or a steeple, (2) an inner chamber where the image of the deity is installed, (3) a hall meant for the audience to sit in, (4) a front porch and (5) a man-made reservoir of fresh water within the temple precincts, if the temple is not close to a natural water source such as a river or a lake. Fresh water is needed to keep the temple floor clean and for temple rituals. The reservoir is also used by some devotees to take a purificatory bath before entering the temple.

Khājurāho Temple

The steeple or the dome is called *shikhara* or summit. The shikhara is meant to represent the mythological mountain Meru, thought to be the highest of all mountains. The inner chamber of the temple is called *garbha-griha*, which literally means "womb-chamber." This chamber resembles a cave. The audience hall is called *nāta-mandira* which means the hall for temple-dancing. In the past, women dancers called *devadāsīs* (handmaids of God) used to perform dance rituals in the audience hall for the entertainment of the deity.

The shikhara, which is the highest point of the temple, symbolizes the worshiper's desire to ascend to the highest peak of spiritual experience. The womb-chamber represents the cave or sanctuary of the worshiper's heart where God has to be made manifest through worship.

Only the temple priests are usually allowed to enter the garbha-griha. Devotees sit in the audience hall, chant the scriptures or the holy name of God, meditate, or simply watch the priests perform the ritualistic worship. The garbha-griha usually does not have any windows. Instead, it has a wide front door, which when left open allows the devotees sitting in the nata-mandira to watch the ritualistic worship being performed in the garbha-griha. In some temples, however, the audience hall is a separate building not connected to the garbha-griha. The audience hall and the garbha-griha usually have images of different deities in niches in their walls.

Some temples have a walkway around the walls of the garbha-griha for circumambulation by devotees. Circumambulation is traditionally done around the deity in a clockwise direction. It is meant to show respect and honor to the deity. On the front porch of some temples a big metallic bell hangs from the ceiling. The devotees usually ring this bell once or twice while entering or leaving the temple.

Vimāna Style Temple

Great variety is noticed in Hindu temple architecture. Some temples are rectangular, some octagonal, some semicircular and others of different shapes and sizes. The shape of the dome also may differ. In South India *vimāna* style domes are used. In North India they are usually of

Some of the temples in India are owned by individual families, but the public usually has access to them. Other temples are owned by non-profit organizations, or religious trusts, as they are called in India. Trustees of the non-profit organizations manage those temples.

The priest's duty is to perform worship rituals on behalf of the temple trustees or the owners of the temple. The worship starts at daybreak and continues intermittently till 9 or 10 o'clock in the evening. During the worship the priest offers various services to God, just as one would do in regard to someone who is highly loved and adored. As the human mind cannot think other than in human terms, God is looked upon as a person—no matter how glorified—and offered food, drink, flowers, perfume, etc. The priest is fully aware that God does not really need any of these things, because He is not wanting in anything. Nevertheless, he offers them to God as a token of his employer's love and adoration. Devotees who are neither owners nor trustees of the temple can also bring food to be offered to the deity. In such cases the priest takes the food from the devotees and offers it to God on their behalf. The consecrated food, called *prasāda*, is freely distributed by the priest—depending on the policy of the temple authorities—to the devotees, wandering monks or nuns, and the poor. Eating prasāda is considered spiritually beneficial; therefore, devotees sometimes go to temples especially for this food. Some temples sell consecrated food to devotees who have not brought any food offering for the deity. It is also a tradition to give the deity a ritual bath every day. The bath water is considered very holy. Small quantities of that water are drunk by devotees for their mental and physical purification. It is stored in a metallic cup inside the temple for their use. This water is called *mahāsnāna-jala* or *charanāmrita* in Sanskrit.

THE ROLE OF TEMPLES IN HINDU SOCIETY

Visiting temples is not obligatory for Hindus. Every Hindu home usually has a shrine, no matter how small, where daily prayers are offered. Hindus generally go to their temples only during important religious festivals. As a result, temples do not have as much hold on Hindus as Christian churches or Jewish synagogues have over their members. They are not the hubs of social activity. Temples usually have religious activities only. Marriages and funeral services, commonly conducted in churches, are not held in Hindu temples. But Hindu temples often organize *kīrtanas* (devotional singing) and religious discourses for the public.

A Gopuram or temple gateway

XIX

THE THREE GUNAS

PRAKRITI OR MOTHER NATURE IS COMPOSED OF THE THREE GUNAS

The concept of the *gunas* plays a very important role in Hinduism. *Guna* usually means quality, but in the context of Hindu philosophy it has another, more technical meaning. This second meaning of the word has its source in the Sānkhya school of philosophy. According to this school, the world has two parts:[1] spirit and matter. The matter part of the world has its source in *Prakriti* or Mother Nature, from which this world has evolved.

Prakriti is composed of three extremely subtle and intangible substances called *sattva, rajas* and *tamas.* If Prakriti is compared to a rope, these three substances constituting Prakriti are its three strands. A strand or a string is called *guna* in Sanskrit. That is why these substances are called *sattva-guna, rajo-guna* and *tamo-guna.*[2]

The spiritual domain of the world, however, contains innumerable sentient entities, each one infinite and perfect. Such an entity is called a *purusha.* What we call in layman's terms a "soul" is called purusha in Sānkhya

---

1. See chapter 20, "Sānkhya Theory of Creation," page 167.
2. According to Sanskrit rules of compounding words, rajas and tamas after combining with the word guna become "rajo" and "tamo," hence, rajo-guna and tamo-guna.

philosophy. There are as many purushas as there are beings in the universe.[3]

THE GUNAS CONSTITUTE THE UNIVERSE

Before the creation of the world, sattva, rajas and tamas remain in a state of perfect equilibrium. If we compare the pre-creation state of Prakriti to a river, then sattva, rajas and tamas are three streams flowing side by side in it. At that state there is perfect harmony between them; they flow without overlapping one another.

When they start intermingling and overlapping, the state of harmony is lost and creation starts.[4] Following an evolutionary process, Prakriti gradually becomes this manifold universe. Everything which exists in this world in the form of matter, energy or mind is no other than an evolved form of Prakriti. As Prakriti is composed of the three gunas, everything in this world is also composed of them. The *Bhagavad Gītā* says (18/40), "There is no such entity in this world, or in heaven, where live the Devas with shiny bodies, which can be free from the three gunas born of Prakriti."

One may wonder how these extremely subtle gunas through the process of evolution can become this gross and tangible world. Its possibility is corroborated by today's physics, which says that something as subtle as energy can be transformed into solid matter. Some physicists also are of the opinion that the primary building blocks of this manifold universe are most probably three types of extremely subtle quarks.

---

3. See page 167.
4. See page 168.

THE EXISTENCE OF THE GUNAS CAN
ONLY BE KNOWN INDIRECTLY

These intangible gunas are so subtle and fine that compared to them even the photons or the sub-atomic particles like electrons and neutrinos are relatively gross. The gunas are finer and subtler than anything that we know of in this world. And yet, according to Sānkhya philosophy, everything in this world is composed of the three gunas.

Their existence cannot be directly perceived because of their extreme subtlety. Just as we cannot see electricity and yet we know its presence by seeing its manifestation in electrical appliances, so also we can know the presence of the gunas indirectly by seeing their various manifestations. Each guna has its own distinctive qualities or characteristics; they manifest themselves through objects in the world. By seeing these characteristics the presence of the gunas can be inferred.

THE CHARACTERISTICS OF THE GUNAS

Sattva-guna is light or buoyant, bright or illuminating. It is of the nature of pleasure or joy; and it has the ability to reveal or make things known. The luminosity of light, the ability of the mind and the senses to know things, the reflecting power of a mirror, and the transparency of glass and crystals are all due to the presence of sattva-guna in them. Similarly, if we see happiness, contentment, satisfaction, joy or bliss in a mind, we should know that it is due to the presence of sattva in it. In the same manner the lightness or buoyancy of cork or similar substances can be explained in terms of the presence of sattva-guna.

Rajo-guna causes activity, movement and restlessness. Avarice, hankering, anger, egoism, vanity, and the wish to dominate over others are also characteristics of rajo-guna. It also is of the nature of pain and suffering; it is the cause of all types of painful experiences. In this world, wherever we see activity, movement or restlessness, pain or suffering, we should know that it is due to rajo-guna.

The characteristics of tamo-guna are inertia, passivity, sluggishness, heaviness and negativity. It resists activity or movement. It renders the mind incapable of knowing things clearly by making it sluggish. It causes confusion, mental depression, bewilderment and ignorance. It induces drowsiness and sleep.

The gunas share one common characteristic. They are in perpetual conflict with one another, each one trying to subdue the others in order to become predominant.[5] At the same time they cooperate with one another. A candle flame exists through the cooperation of the wick, wax and fire. The flame will cease to exist without such cooperation. Similarly, the world exists owing to the cooperation of the three gunas. Before creation the gunas remain in a state of perfect equilibrium with none of them claiming preponderance. After the dissolution of the world, they regain that original state of equilibrium. But it is lost when the next cycle of creation begins (see page 165).

GOD-VISION IS POSSIBLE WITH THE HELP OF SATTVA-GUNA

A preponderance of sattva-guna is conducive to a person's spiritual growth. One endowed with a predomi-

---

5. *Bhagavad Gītā* 14/10.

nance of sattva-guna acquires a divine nature and is blessed with God-vision. According to the *Bhagavad Gītā*, such a person is fearless, is of pure mind, has steadfast knowledge about his inherent divine Self, has control over his external organs, is fond of scriptural study, has mental and physical endurance, and is straightforward at all times. Non-injury, truthfulness, absence of anger, renunciation of sensual pleasures, absence of the habit of vilification, kindness to creatures, non-covetousness, gentleness, modesty, lack of restlessness, vigor, forgiveness, fortitude, freedom from malice, and absence of haughtiness are the other qualities of a person endowed with a preponderance of sattva-guna.[6]

Sattva-guna gives spiritual liberation. Rajo-guna causes bondage through attachment to action.[7] Tamo-guna causes confused thinking or senseless violence. The following parable of Shrī Rāmakrishna beautifully expresses these ideas.

As a rich man was passing through a forest one day, he fell into the hands of three robbers, who stole all his money. Then one of the robbers said, "What's the use of keeping this man alive? Let's kill him." Saying this, the robber was about to kill the man with his sword, when the second robber said, "There's no point in killing him unnecessarily. Let's tie his hands and feet and leave him here. Then he won't be able to tell the police." Accordingly, the robbers tied the man with a rope and, leaving him there, went away.

After a while the third robber returned to the man and said, "I'm sorry you had to go through all this trouble.

6. *Bhagavad Gītā* 16/1, 16/2, 16/3 & 16/5.
7. *Bhagavad Gītā* 14/7.

Come, I'm going to release you." He then set the rich man free and led him out of the forest. When they came near the highway, the robber said, "Follow this road; this will lead you to your village." The rich man felt grateful and invited the robber to come with him to his home. But the robber said, "It's not possible for me to go there. There is a police station in your village; if I go there the police will arrest me." So saying, the robber went away.

The first robber, who wanted to kill the rich man, is tamo-guna. Tamo-guna creates confused thinking and causes unnecessary violence. The second robber is rajo-guna, which binds a man to the world and entangles him in numerous activities. Rajo-guna makes a person forget God. The third robber represents sattva-guna. Sattva-guna alone shows the way to God and causes liberation from the bondage of the world. For the rich man arriving home is like reaching God. Sattva-guna can lead a person to God, but it itself cannot go there. God, being Spirit, is beyond matter or the three gunas. This explains why the third robber could not go to the rich man's home.

LIBERATED SOULS GO BEYOND THE THREE GUNAS

To attain spiritual liberation, a spiritual aspirant has to transcend these three gunas. In the *Bhagavad Gīta* Shrī Krishna, a Divine Incarnation, says to his student Arjuna, "Go beyond the three gunas."[8] In other words, go beyond matter and manifest your divine spirit.

---

8. *Bhagavad Gītā* 2/45.

XX

CREATION

INTRODUCTION

Hinduism presents more than one theory about the creation of this world. The various schools of Hindu religious philosophy, such as Sānkhya, Vaisheshika, Mīmāmsā, Vedānta and others, have different theories about creation. Sānkhya, Yoga, Nyāya, Vaisheshika and Vedānta consider creation to be both beginningless and endless, and have the concept of an infinite series of successive creations and dissolutions of the world.[1] Before creation the entire world remains in a potential state or seed-form in God. This is called the *avyakta* or unmanifested state of the world. The world becomes manifest when God projects the world out of Himself. The world after manifestation or creation still remains inside God and undergoes a process of evolution. The evolved world is allowed to exist for a certain length of time, lasting billions of years, until God decides to withdraw it back into Himself. After its withdrawal the world goes back again to its seed or unmanifested state. The projection of the world, its temporary existence, and its withdrawal back into God comprise a *kalpa* or a cycle.[2]

---

1. The Sanskrit words for creation and dissolution are *srishti* and *pralaya* respectively.
2. The Sānkhya school, which is atheistic, has a different concept of creation, but it accepts the kalpa theory of creation.

An analogy will make this idea clear. Let us suppose a man goes to his doctor for his annual checkup. An X-ray shows that a benign tumor is forming inside his stomach. The tumor grows bigger and bigger until it becomes as large as a chicken egg and stays that way for a while. Then, without any treatment, the tumor gradually shrinks and disappears completely.

In this particular analogy the man represents God and his tumor symbolizes the world. Just as after its projection from God the world goes on evolving inside Him and eventually is withdrawn back into Him, so also the tumor appears inside the man's body, starts evolving and getting bigger inside him, and eventually goes back to where it came from. The appearance of the tumor, its gradual growth and continuance, and its final disappearance symbolically constitute a kalpa or a cycle. According to Hinduism, there is an infinite series of such cycles or kalpas. That is why creation is thought to be without any beginning or end in Hinduism. Every kalpa is believed to be identical to the other kalpas either preceding or succeeding it.

Questions have been raised in Hinduism about God's motive for creation. Every action is prompted by a sense of want. As God is not wanting in anything, why should He act? Or, in other words, why should He create? One scriptural text gives a rather poetic reply to this question, as though echoing the voice of God, saying, "I shall be many. May I manifest Myself numerously."[3] This means that God, even though the one and only reality, wanted to "become" this manifold universe; hence the creation.

---

3. In Sanskrit *bahu syām prajāyeyeti* (*Chhāndogya Upanishad* 6.2.3)

His wish to become this world was not generated by any "real" feeling of want. From His standpoint creation is only a "game," or *līlā*.[4]

Has God really become the world? In reply to this question some schools of Hindu philosophy say that God has *really* become this manifold universe, just as milk really becomes yogurt. Other schools say that God only *appears* to have become this world; He has not really become the world. A rope in partial darkness may appear to become a snake to an observer, so also God has apparently become the world. He has not really transformed Himself into the world.

Hinduism, as a religion, has the unique ability to accommodate both theistic and atheistic ideas. For instance, the Sānkhya school of Hindu philosophy, which is atheistic, is accepted by Hinduism side by side with other schools of philosophy which believe in the existence of God. The Sānkhya system, although atheistic, can help people attain spiritual liberation. How the Sānkhya system explains the creation of this world in the absence of a creator God may be of interest to readers.

Sānkhya theory of creation

The Sānkhya system is the most ancient of all the schools of Hindu philosophy. This system recognizes two types of ultimate reality: (1) *Purusha* and (2) *Prakriti*.

Purusha is pure consciousness or pure sentience. It is uncaused, changeless, eternal and all-pervading. It is pure spirit, and as such it is totally devoid of matter. It is also entirely passive. There are innumerable Purushas.

---

4. This Sanskrit word *līlā* means "play acting" or "play."

There are as many Purushas as there are conscious beings. Objections have been raised by other schools about the Sānkhya concept of many Purushas. According to them, since Purusha is all-pervading, the idea of many Purushas occupying the same space is not acceptable. The Sānkhya reply to this objection is that Purushas have no difficulty coexisting, just as the light from different candles can occupy the same space without any conflict. The Sānkhya school also argues in favor of the plurality of Purushas by pointing out that had there been only one Purusha, the birth or death of one conscious being would also cause the birth and death of all other conscious beings. But that is not the case. Therefore, there must be many Purushas.

Prakriti, as opposed to Purusha, is unconscious primordial matter. Even though Prakriti is uncaused, it is the cause of everything in this universe, whether matter, energy, or even mind. Hindu psychology very clearly states that mind, no matter how subtle, is no other than a material substance. It also should be remembered here that Purusha, being pure spirit, has not been caused by Prakriti.

According to the Sānkhya school, Prakriti is composed of three extremely subtle substances called sattva, rajas and tamas. The process of creation starts when Prakriti borrows consciousness from Purusha and starts acting like a conscious entity. The first sign of Prakriti's conscious activity is seen in its tendency to change itself. It undergoes a process of gradual transformation, the final outcome of which is this manifold world. In other words, primordial matter, Prakriti, becomes the world through a process of evolution.

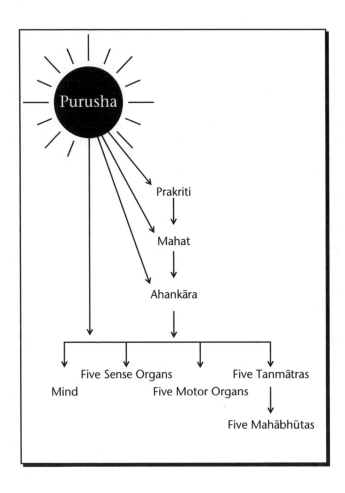

The Process of Creation (Sānkhya School)

170 THE ESSENTIALS OF HINDUISM

The first product of the evolution of Prakriti is *Mahat* or cosmic intellect. *Ahankāra* or cosmic ego is the second product of Prakriti.

There are three types of cosmic ego: (1) ego in which the Sattva substance is predominant, (2) ego in which the Rajas substance is preponderant and (3) ego with the preponderance of Tamas substance. From the first are evolved the five sense organs, the five motor organs and the mind. From the third are evolved the five subtle physical essences or *tanmātras*. The second—that in which Rajas is predominant—provides the energy to the first and the third to evolve.

From the tanmātras are evolved the five gross physical elements or *mahābhūtas*: (1) *ākāsha*—the space element, (2) *vāyu*—the air element, (3) *agni*—the fire element, (4) *ap*—the water element, (5) *kshiti or prithivī*—the earth element. These elements mingle in different proportions following certain rules of permutation and combination and become the manifold universe.[5]

Creation according to the Vedānta school of philosophy

The non-dualistic school of Vedānta philosophy accepts God as the creator of this world. But it holds the view that the world is only an apparent transformation of God.

An analogy is used by the non-dualistic school of Vedānta philosophy to explain how God has created this world. Let us suppose a magician has cast a hypnotic spell on his audience. By hypnotic suggestion he creates

5. S. Chatterjee & D. Datta, *An Introduction To Indian Philosophy*, 7th ed. (Calcutta, India: University Of Calcutta, 1968), 267–274.

an apple tree on the stage. The entire audience will see
that apple tree, but not the magician, since he is not
under the spell of his own hypnotic power. Similarly,
God (Īshvara), using His power of magic or *māyā*, has created this world. This world is real to those who are under
the spell of God's māyā. It is not real to God. From His
standpoint He has not *really* created the world. To us who
are under the sway of His māyā the world appears to be
real. And, from our point of view, God the Creator also
seems to be real. The *Creation Hymn* of the *Rig-Veda* beautifully expresses this idea:

> Not non-existent was it nor existent was it
> at that time;
> There was not atmosphere nor the heavens
> which are beyond.
> What existed? Where? In whose care?
> Water was it? An abyss unfathomable?

> Neither mortal was there
> nor immortal then;
> Not of night, of day was there distinction:
> *That* alone breathed windless
> through inherent power.
> Other than *That* there was naught else.

> Darkness it was, by darkness hidden
> in the beginning:
> an undistinguished sea was all this.
> The germ of all things which was
> enveloped in void,
> *That* alone through the power
> of brooding thought was born.

> Upon *That* in the beginning arose desire,
> which was the first offshoot of that thought.
> This desire sages found out to be the link

between the existent and the non-existent,
after searching with the wisdom in their heart.

Straight across was extended their line of vision:
was *That* below, was *That* above?
Seed-placers there were, powers there were:
potential energy below, impulse above.

Who, after all, knows?
Who here will declare whence it arose,
whence this world?
Subsequent are the gods
to the creation of this world.
Who then, knows whence it came into being?

This world—whence it came into being,
whether it was made or whether not—
He who is the overseer in the highest heavens
surely knows—
or perhaps He knows not![6]

In the above Rig-Vedic hymn doubts have been raised
in the last stanza about the *real* creation of this world.
The "overseer in the highest heavens" is no other than
Īshvara or God the Creator. He is all-knowing. He must
know if the world has been created. If He does not know,
then it may mean that from His point of view no world
has really been created. For what is not really there, the
question of knowing its existence cannot arise. Therefore,
it does not contradict Īshvara's omniscience.

Nevertheless, from the point of view of mortals under
the sway of māyā (God's power of creating illusion), the
world is real, and it must have a cause or a Creator. From

---

6. Walter H. Maurer, trans., *Pinnacles Of India's Past, Selections
from the Rgveda* (Amsterdam/Philadelphia: John Benjamins Publishing Company, 1986), 283–284.

their standpoint, God by mere thought created the first being called Hiranyagarbha. Even though created by God, Hiranyagarbha is endowed with almost divine powers. He has infinite powers of knowledge, will and action. Through meditation Hiranyagarbha comes to know everything about the previous kalpa or cycle. Then by his thought he creates the rest of the world exactly following the order of the previous kalpa.

First *ākāsha* or the space element is created. Then in succession are created *vāyu* the air element, *agni* the fire element, *ap* the water element, and *prithivī* the earth element. In Sanskrit, something which has come into being is called a *bhūta*, and these five manifested elements are called *bhūtas*. These elements are extremely subtle. The Sanskrit counterparts of the words *five* and *subtle* are respectively *pancha* and *sūkshma*. Therefore, these five subtle elements are called *Pancha sūkshma-bhūtas*.[7]

These five subtle elements then mingle together in five different ways to produce the five gross (in Sanskrit: sthūla) elements. These five gross elements are called *pancha sthūla-bhūtas*. The process of mixing the five subtle elements to produce the five gross elements is called *panchīkarana* in Sanskrit. The process of such mixing is given below:

½ subtle space + ⅛ subtle air + ⅛ subtle fire + ⅛ subtle water + ⅛ subtle earth produce "gross" space element.

½ subtle air + ⅛ subtle space + ⅛ subtle fire + ⅛ subtle water + ⅛ subtle earth produce "gross" air element.

½ subtle fire + ⅛ subtle space + ⅛ subtle air + ⅛ subtle water + ⅛ subtle earth produce "gross" fire element.

---

7. They are also called *tanmātras*.

½ subtle water + ⅛ subtle space + ⅛ subtle air + ⅛ subtle fire + ⅛ subtle earth produce "gross" water element.

½ subtle earth + ⅛ subtle space + ⅛ subtle air + ⅛ subtle fire + ⅛ subtle water produce "gross" earth element.

The subtle body of man is made of the five subtle elements, and his gross body and all gross objects of nature arise by the mixture of the five gross elements.

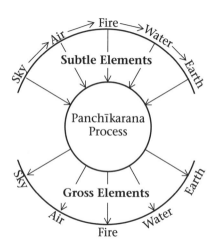

The Evolution of the Gross Elements from the Subtle Elements (Vedānta School)

PRALAYA OR THE DISSOLUTION OF THE WORLD

As a created being, no matter how glorified or endowed with power, Hiranyagarbha has limited longevity. One day of his life, called a *kalpa*, is equal to 4,320,000,000 human years, and he lives for 100 years according to this time scale.[8] According to another view one kalpa consists of 8,640,000,000 human years.[9] The life span of Hiranyagarbha is called a *mahā-kalpa* (36,500 kalpas).[10]

When Hiranyagarbha goes to sleep after his day's work, there is cosmic dissolution or *pralaya*. This is called *naimittika pralaya*. When he wakes up, the creation of the world starts all over again. This process of alternate creation and dissolution continues until Hiranyagarbha dies at the end of the mahā-kalpa.

When Hiranyagarbha dies, he merges into God and becomes one with Him. In other words, he becomes liberated and will not be born again. At the death or liberation of Hiranyagarbha the world undergoes dissolution, which is called *prākrita pralaya*, and the mahā-kalpa ends.

By the will of God when the next cycle of creation starts, another exalted mortal being appears as Hiranyagarbha by virtue of the extraordinary merits earned by him in the previous kalpa or cycle of creation. Thus the process of repeated creation, continuance and dissolution of the universe goes on forever.

AN OBJECTION REGARDING THE HINDU THEORIES OF CREATION & ITS REFUTATION

It may seem that Hindu cosmogony is not sure about the origin of this world. Had it been sure, it would have

---

8. John Dowson, *A Classical Dictionary of Hindu Mythology and Religion, Geography, History and Literature* (London: Routledge & Kegan Paul Ltd., 1953), 145.
9. John Grimes, *A Concise Dictionary of Indian Philosophy* (Albany: State University of New York Press, 1989), 166.
10. Amal Bandopadhyay, *Pauranika*, vol. I (Calcutta: Firma K.L.M. Pr. Ltd.,1978), 248–249.

offered only one theory of creation. As it presents more than one theory, one may argue that either all the theories are wrong, or only one is correct.

Yet such an objection does not pose any problem for the non-dualistic school of Vedānta philosophy. Shankara, the great saint and non-dualist philosopher of India, says that this world has empirical existence, but no ultimate existence. In other words, the world is real for the time being only; it is not ultimately real. In the final analysis when the unreality of the world is established, every theory of creation will automatically be proved to be invalid and meaningless. Therefore, it does not matter if there are numerous theories or just one theory about creation.

To understand Shankara's non-dualistic position, one should be acquainted with the meaning of the word "real" in Hindu philosophy. According to Hindu philosophy, whatever is *real* must be *eternal* and *changeless*.

For instance, if someone saw a dinosaur appear in his backyard, stay there for one minute, and then suddenly vanish into thin air, he would realize that what he saw was not real. He would realize that his sighting of the dinosaur must have been caused by either an optical illusion or his heightened imagination. On the other hand, had the dinosaur existed forever, it would be considered real by him. In that case his judgment of the "reality" of the dinosaur would be based on its perpetuity.

Now let us suppose that an observer is seeing a creature which keeps on changing its form every minute. The first minute it is a dog, then it becomes a weasel, then a racoon, and then something else. Owing to its ever changing nature the observer is not able to determine the true identity of the creature; he does not know what it "really" is. Had the creature not changed at all, there would be no difficulty in ascertaining the true or "real" identity of the creature. It would be known in terms of the "changelessness" of the creature.

The world has a beginning in time. Therefore, it cannot be eternal; it must be transitory. Being transitory it cannot be real. The unreality of the world can also be determined by its ever-changing character.

To explain the illusory and unreal character of the world, Shankara uses the analogy of a rope, which when seen in the dark, is seen as a snake. The "reality" is the rope, but it is being observed as a snake. As long as the illusion lasts, the so-called snake seems to be real. When the darkness goes, the so-called snake disappears. The observer comes to realize that even though the snake appeared to exist for a while, it actually was *never* there.

According to Shankara, the rope represents Nirguna Brahman or Impersonal God, and the snake represents the world. Nirguna Brahman, being eternal and changeless, is the only reality that exists. To a person who has come to know Nirguna Brahman, the world is not real to him anymore. He also comes to know that the world was never created. Therefore, the question about the origin or creation of an "uncreated" world cannot arise.

XXI

MOKSHA OR LIBERATION FROM SAMSĀRA

INTRODUCTION

The derivative meaning of the Sanskrit word *samsāra* is "the repeated passing of souls through different worlds— gross or subtle." In other words, samsāra means going through the cycle of repeated births and deaths. According to Hinduism the goal of human life is to be free or liberated from repeated births and deaths. Such liberation is called *moksha* or *mukti* in Sanskrit. Moksha can be attained only through God-realization.

The various schools of Hindu philosophy (*darshana*) hold differing views about moksha. Some schools say that moksha can be achieved by people only after their death, others claim that it can be achieved even while they are alive. There are also differences of opinion regarding the nature of moksha. The following paragraphs will introduce the reader to these views and concepts.

MOKSHA ACCORDING TO THE *DVAITA* SCHOOL OF PHILOSOPHY

The *Dvaita,* or dualistic school of Vedānta philosophy, believes in post-mortem liberation only. A person who has gone through rigorous ethical and moral disciplines followed by right knowledge, right action, non-attachment, and devotional meditation on the Personal God (Vishnu), becomes fit for release or moksha through Īshwara's loving grace. According to this school, there are four gradations or levels of moksha: (1) *sālokya*, (2) *sāmīpya* or *sānnidhya*, (3) *sārūpya*, and (4) *sāyujya*. Among the four, the first one is the lowest and the last one is the highest. Depending upon his spiritual progress the departed soul may achieve any one of the four kinds of moksha.

In sālokya-mukti the departed soul goes to *ishta-loka* (the abode of the Personal God, such as the abode of Vishnu), and stays there blissfully enjoying His presence; in sāmīpya or sānnidhya-mukti the departed soul enjoys the bliss of extreme proximity to the Personal God; in sārūpya-mukti the departed soul acquires the form of the Personal God and enjoys intense bliss; in sāyujya-mukti the departed soul becomes blissfully absorbed in the Personal God.

MOKSHA ACCORDING TO THE *ADVAITA* SCHOOL OF PHILOSOPHY

The *Advaita*, or non-dualistic school of Vedānta philosophy, believes that one can have liberation from samsāra even when alive. Such release or liberation is called *jīvanmukti* in Sanskrit. According to this school, a spiritual aspirant has to first go through various moral and ethical practices, worship (upāsanā) of the Personal God, etc. These observances gradually purifiy his mind and make it ready for intense meditation on the Impersonal Divine Reality (*Nirguna Brahman*). Such meditation enables him to have *ātmajnāna* or the knowledge of his inner Divine

Self. Ātmajnāna destroys the mantle of ignorance (*avidyā*) that covers the knowledge of the Reality. Release will come as soon as his ignorance is annihilated. Then he becomes a *jīvanmukta* (one who has had jīvanmukti). After attaining jīvanmukti he can no longer think of himself as an embodied being. To a jīvanmukta, the body—like the rest of the world—appears illusory. The illusory body of the jīvanmukta continues to exist as long as his prārabdha karma lasts. When the prārabdha is exhausted and the illusory body dies, the jīvanmukta attains his disembodied release called *videha-mukti.*

According to one view, a jīvanmukta may totally lose interest in his illusory body *immediately* after attaining jīvanmukti. As a result, his body drops off in a matter of days causing his *sadyomukti* or "immediate release."[1]

Other scholars say that the term jīvanmukti, from the standpoint of those who have attained ātmajnāna, means sadyomukti or immediate liberation. After attaining ātmajnāna, these liberated souls can no longer identify with their bodies, which along with the rest of the world have become illusory and unreal. So far as they are concerned, their bodies are not *really* there. Therefore, from

---

1. Committing suicide by a spiritually unenlightened person is condemned by Hinduism because it causes him intense after-death suffering. However, according to the scriptures, a jīvanmukta whose lack of interest in his body causes its death is not adversely affected by the loss of his body. According to Shrī Rāmakrishna, most of those who attain jīvanmukti through nirvikalpa samādhi cannot bring down their minds anymore to the plane of this earthly existence. Their minds remain immersed in Brahman-consciousness. In that state they totally lose their body-consciousness. As a result, their bodies cannot get nourishment and drop off after a few days.

their standpoint they have attained sadyomukti. However, observers who see such souls may call them jīvan-muktas.

There is another concept about liberation called *krama-mukti* or *avāntara-mukti* (liberation through stages). According to this concept, a person who has intensely meditated on Saguna Brahman using the sacred sound symbol Aum or other prescribed methods of meditation such as dahara-vidyā, shāndilya-vidyā, etc., goes to Brahma-loka after death. There he attains the knowledge of Nirguna Brahman under the guidance of Hiranyagarbha. When the entire universe is dissolved at the end of the kalpa he becomes one with Brahman and is not born again. This type of liberation from samsāra is called krama-mukti or avāntara-mukti.

MOKSHA ACCORDING TO THE
VISHISHTĀDVAITA SCHOOL OF PHILOSOPHY

The *Vishishtādvaita*, or school of qualified non-dualism of Vedānta philosophy, does not accept the idea of jīvan-mukti. A person can be liberated only after his death. Moksha means living blissfully in *vaikuntha*, which is the realm of the Personal God. A person who has attained moksha lives blissfully in vaikuntha in a spiritual body in the presence of God. He acquires many divine powers such as omniscience, etc., but unlike God he cannot create, sustain or dissolve the world. In spite of his exalted state he has to remain subservient to God.

According to this school, liberation cannot be attained by ātmajnāna as is maintained by the Advaita system. This school also says that Karma Yoga and Jnāna Yoga are only aids to Bhakti Yoga. One can be liberated from the bondage of this samsāra only through God's grace. Bhakti Yoga practices are the only means of obtaining divine grace.

MOKSHA ACCORDING TO THE
SĀNKHYA SCHOOL OF PHILOSOPHY

In this system, the soul or the spirit is *purusha*, and the body-mind complex is an evolved form of unconscious primordial matter, *prakriti*. Purusha is pure consciousness; prakriti, although inherently unconscious, functions by borrowing consciousness from purusha. The bondage of purusha is caused by *aviveka* or purusha's false identification with prakriti and its evolved products like mind, body, etc. Such false identification is caused by purusha's ignorance. While in bondage, purusha suffers mental and physical pain because of its false identification with the body-mind complex. In order to get rid of this false identification and consequent pain and suffering, purusha must acquire the knowledge that, as spirit, it is completely different and distinct from prakriti and its evolved product—the body-mind complex. This knowledge is called *viveka-jnāna*. In the Sānkhya system, moksha (also called *kaivalya*) means the complete cessation of suffering and pain. It is viveka-jnāna which causes purusha's moksha by disentangling purusha from prakriti.

The Sānkhya system, like the Advaita system, accepts the idea of jīvanmukti or emancipation of the soul while living in the body. When a jīvanmukta dies, he attains videha-mukti.

MOKSHA ACCORDING TO THE *PŪRVA-MĪMĀMSĀ* SCHOOL OF PHILOSOPHY

This school believes only in after-death liberation of the soul. It does not believe in jīvanmukti. Moksha can be achieved through the right performance of rituals as enjoined by the Vedas. The concept of moksha in the early Pūrva-Mīmāmsā system is that the liberated soul goes to heaven and enjoys heavenly bliss forever. But the later Pūrva-Mīmāmsā school describes moksha as a state devoid of the possibility of rebirth, and thus free from the possibility of consequent pain and suffering. It does not speak of moksha as a state of heavenly bliss.

MOKSHA ACCORDING TO THE *NYĀYA* AND THE *VAISHESHIKA* SCHOOLS OF PHILOSOPHY

These two schools are similar in their concept of Moksha. These schools say that liberation (Apavarga) is a separation from all qualities. Liberation is a state beyond pleasure, happiness, pain, or any experience whatsoever. It is achieved by cultivating ethical virtues and acquiring the right knowledge of reality. After liberation there is no rebirth.

XXII

CONCLUDING REMARKS

HINDUISM IS REALISTIC—IT IS NEITHER OPTIMISTIC NOR PESSIMISTIC

Some scholars are of the opinion that Hinduism is a pessimistic religion. According to them, Hinduism has a pessimistic view towards this world, tending to put more emphasis on the other world, ignoring the world we live in. But the most authentic scriptures of Hinduism, such as the *Rig-Veda* and the *Yajur-Veda*, give us a completely different view. We come to know from them that the Aryans of the Vedic period enjoyed a very high standard of material comfort. To them this world was good and enjoyable; it was not evil. According to the *Īsha Upanishad*, "(man) should wish to live for one hundred years." The Aryans wore fine clothes and gold jewelry, enjoyed music, dancing, good food and wine. Milk cows, their main wealth, were numerous. There is mention of heaven but practically no mention of hell.[1]

An unbiased study of Hinduism reveals that it is neither pessimistic nor overly optimistic. Too much optimism causes frequent disappointments, while pessimism robs

1. See the article "The Vedic Culture" by C. Kunhan Raja, D. Phil. (Oxon), Head of the Department of Sanskrit, Madras University, in the book *The Cultural Heritage Of India, Vol. I*, published by the Ramakrishna Mission Institue of Culture, Gol Park, Calcutta.

people of their initiative. Neither is encouraged by Hinduism. Hinduism is purely realistic. It encourages its followers to recognize the true nature of the world and act accordingly.

Hindu scriptures speak of two goals pursued by man: (1) the pleasant and (2) the good. What is pleasant may not necessarily be good, and what is good may not be pleasant. Besides, that which is pleasant now may become unpleasant later. Eating a chocolate cupcake may be a pleasant experience, but if a person is forced at gunpoint to eat eight chocolate cupcakes in quick succession, it becomes torture. To an alcoholic, drinking liquor may be pleasant, but it certainly is not good for him. Getting daily physical exercise is not necessarily pleasant, but it is undoubtedly good for one's health. Similarly, certain mental and physical indulgences may be pleasant, but they are neither good for the body nor the mind. Hinduism asks its followers to give up such indulgences. It does not encourage its followers to live in an unreal fantasy world where bad is painted as good, and what is harmful is imagined as beneficial simply because it is pleasant. It exhorts its followers to be realistic and hold on to what is good, giving up what may be pleasant but not good.

HINDUISM IS NOT FATALISTIC

Hinduism does not believe in fatalism. According to the doctrine of karma, a person's future is his or her own creation. The good or bad actions done in the present will cause enjoyment or suffering in the future. To create a better future one must wisely utilize the present moment by performing good activities. Blaming someone else for one's own suffering is not condoned by Hinduism. The worker must take full responsibility for his or her good or bad actions and consequent pleasure or pain.

HINDUISM'S POSITION IN REGARD TO MORTIFICATION OF THE BODY

Purposeless and neurotic mortification of the body is not encouraged by mainstream Hinduism.[2] Physical austerity is necessary as much as it helps to strengthen the mind. A person who is not easily affected by heat or cold, pleasure or pain, is mentally a stronger person. He is more likely to handle the various problems in his life without being defeated by them. Too much identification with the body makes a person mentally weak. Hinduism clearly forbids its followers to go to any extreme.[3] Neglecting the body is not considered necessarily a virtue. *Sharīramādyam khalu dharmasādhanam*—"The body is the primary instrument to practice religion or dharma"— says Hinduism. The body therefore has to be taken care of. Hindu scriptures also teach that the body is the temple of God, because the soul or the indwelling Divine Self resides in it.

IDEA AND PRACTICE OF NONVIOLENCE IN HINDUISM

Although Hinduism considers nonviolence the greatest virtue, it is not blind to the fact that we must put up with

---

2. The *Bhagavad Gītā* 17/6 says, "Those who, being non-discriminating, torture all the organs in the body as also even Me (i.e. God) who reside in the body—know them as possessed of demonical conviction."

3. The Sanskrit saying *sarvam atyanta garhitam* means "too much of anything is bad."

one or another kind of violence merely to survive.[4] Thousands of microscopic lives are destroyed every time we breathe. Each food grain we eat has life in it. It is impossible to completely avoid committing violence. All that Hinduism expects its followers to do is to consciously minimize violence as much as is practicable to get rid of the violent attitude of mind.

However, violence justified by a noble cause may sometimes be condoned by Hinduism. Such justification must come from the dictates of the scriptures; not from any other source. If an enemy attacks a country, the soldiers must fight in order to repel, subdue or kill that enemy. It is the religious duty of the soldiers to defend the country. Killing a fleeing, wounded, defenseless, or incapacitated enemy is not permitted by the scriptures. A soldier who escapes from the battlefield out of fright, and wants to justify his cowardice by extolling the virtue of nonviolence, has failed in his duty and is a hypocrite.

Ideally speaking, a truly nonviolent person is not supposed to hurt anyone by his body, mind or speech. Total nonviolence is possible for a spiritually-illumined soul only. Such a soul loses his false identification with his body-mind complex and comes to know his true divine identity. He experiences God as the essence of all things and all beings, including himself. Therefore, he cannot hate or harm anyone.

He alone can love his enemies, because he does not see an enemy anywhere. All that he experiences is the

---

4. *Ahimsaiva hi sarvebhyo dharmebhyo jyāyasī matā*—"Nonviolence is considered the greatest of all virtues." *Mahābhārata* (Shāntiparva) 257/6.

manifestation of God. As he can no longer identify with his psycho-physical complex, he cannot hold himself responsible for whatever his body or mind does. He loses his sense of agency, the awareness that he is the doer of things. Thus, he goes beyond violence. The *Bhagavad Gītā* (18/17) says, "He who does not have the sense of agency or egoism, whose intellect does not hold itself responsible for action performed by the body and the senses, he does not kill, nor does he become bound by the result of such killing."[5]

THE IDEA OF THE HARMONY OF RELIGIONS IS INHERENT IN HINDUISM

The spirit of religious tolerance in Hinduism is rooted in this statement from the *Rig-Veda, Ekam sad viprā bahudhā vadanti*—"One (God) alone exists. Sages call *That* by different names." The idea that God can be realized through different spiritual paths has been taught through the ages by many saints and godmen of India. But the idea that all religions lead to the same God is mainly the contribution of the 19th century Hindu saint Shrī Rāmakrishna. He is known as the prophet of the harmony of religions. No book on Hinduism can be written today without acknowledging his contribution. Some of his relevant teachings are recorded below with the hope that they may help, no matter in what small way, in promoting peace and understanding between the religious people of our strife-torn world.

---

5. It has to be understood that a person in such an exalted spiritual state can never "consciously" kill or commit violence.

Shrī Rāmakrishna

Many are the names of God and infinite are the forms through which He may be approached. In whatever name and form you worship Him, through that you will realize Him.

God has made different religions to suit different aspirants, times and countries. All doctrines are so many paths; but a path is by no means God Himself. Indeed, one can reach God if one follows any of the paths with whole hearted devotion. One may eat a pastry with icing either straight or sidewise. It will taste sweet either way.

A truly religious man should think that other religions are also so many paths leading to the Truth. One should always maintain an attitude of respect towards other religions.

Different creeds are but different paths to reach the same God.

Various types of jewelry are made of gold. Although they are made of the same substance they have different forms, and they are given different names. So also the one and the same God is worshiped in different countries under different names and forms.

Every man should follow his own religion. A Christian should follow Christianity, a Muslim should follow Islam, and so on. For a Hindu, the ancient path, the path of the Aryan sages, is the best.

Dispute not. As you rest firmly on your own faith and opinion, allow others also the equal liberty to stand by their own

*faiths and opinions. By mere disputation you will never suc-
ceed in convincing another of his error. When the grace of God
descends, each one will understand his own mistakes.*

*God Himself has provided different forms of worship. He
who is the Lord of the Universe has arranged all these forms to
suit different men in different stages of knowledge. The mother
cooks different dishes to suit the stomachs of her children.
Suppose she has five children. If there is a fish to cook, she pre-
pares various dishes from it—pilau, pickled fish, fried fish,
and so on—to suit their different tastes and powers of diges-
tion.*

*God is formless and yet He can assume forms. One monk
went to visit the temple of Lord Jagannath in the holy city of
Puri. While inside the temple, doubts came to his mind. He
started wondering if God had form, or He was formless. As he
was a wandering monk, he was carrying a staff in his hand.
With his staff he wanted to touch the image of Lord Jagannath. He put one end of his staff to the left of the image and
moved it to the right. The staff passed unobstructed through
the image, as if it was not there. But when he tried to move
the staff from right to left, the image obstructed it. Thus, he
realized that God is formless and yet He can have form.*

*A man went to a forest. There, for the first time in his life,
he saw a chameleon sitting on a tree. Later he said to someone, "Brother, in that forest I saw a strange creature on a tree.
It's red in color." The other man said, "I've also seen that creature, it certainly isn't red. It's green." Another person said,
"Why should it be green? I've seen it too, it's yellow." Someone
else claimed that it was violet, while others insisted that it
was either blue or black. Thus they started quarreling. Then
they decided to go back to that tree and found a man sitting
under it. That man said, "I live under this tree; I know this*

creature very well. What you all have been saying is quite true. It is sometimes red, sometimes green, sometimes yellow and sometimes blue." One who contemplates God all the time—he alone knows what God is really like. He alone knows that God reveals Himself in so many different ways. God sometimes assumes different forms. Sometimes He has attributes, sometimes none. One who lives under the tree alone knows that the chameleon has many colors. He also knows that sometimes it doesn't have any color at all. Others who don't know, quarrel and suffer unnecessarily. God has form, then again He is formless. He is like the infinite ocean. The cooling influence of the spiritual aspirant's devotion for God causes the water to freeze and become ice. But when the sun of true knowledge rises, the ice melts and becomes formless water again.

Appendix A

WORLD THINKERS ON HINDUISM AND INDIAN CULTURE

Arthur Schopenhauer (1788–1860), German philosopher, said about the Upanishadic scriptures of Hinduism: "In the whole world there is no study...so beneficial and so elevating as that of the Upanishad. It has been the solace of my life; it will be the solace of my death."

Ralph Waldo Emerson (1803–1882), renowned American poet, essayist and philosopher, wrote: "In all nations there are minds which incline to dwell in the conception of the fundamental Unity. The raptures of prayer and ecstasy of devotion lose all being in one Being. This tendency finds its highest expression in the religious writings of the East and chiefly in the Indian scriptures, in the Vedas, the Bhagavat Geeta, and the Vishnu Purana."

The famous American essayist, poet and naturalist *Henry David Thoreau* (1817–1862) wrote: "What extracts from the Vedas I have read fall on me like light of a higher and purer luminary, which describes a loftier course through a purer stratum—free from particulars, simple, universal. It rises on me like the full moon after the stars have come out, wading through some far summer stratum of the sky."

Friedrich Max M. Müller (1823–1900), the famous philologist and mythologist of England, said: "If one would ask me under what sky the human mind has most fully

193

developed its precious gifts, has scrutinized most pro-foundly the greatest problems of life, and has, at least for some, provided solutions which deserve to be admired even by those who have studied Plato and Kant, I would indicate India.

"And if one would ask me which literature would give us back (us Europeans, who have been exclusively fed on Greek and Roman thought...) the necessary equilibrium in order to make our inner life more perfect, more com-prehensive, more universal, in short, more human, a life not only for this life, but for a transformed and eternal life, once again I would indicate India."

He also said: "Philosophy in India is what it ought to be, not the denial, but the fulfillment of religion; it is the highest religion; and the oldest name of the oldest system of philosophy in India is Vedanta, that is, the end, the goal, the highest object of the Vedas."

The well-known British historian *Arnold Joseph Toynbee* (1889–1975) said: "At this supremely dangerous moment in human history, the only way of salvation is the Indian way. The Emperor Ashoka's and the Mahatma Gandhi's principle of non-violence and Sri Ramakrishna's testi-mony to the harmony of religions; here we have the atti-tude and the spirit that can make it possible for the human race to grow together into a single family...."

Appendix B

MAJOR HINDU RELIGIOUS FESTIVALS

Deepāvalī or Diwālī: Autumn festival of lights. Observed all over India.

Mahā-Shivarātri: Nocturnal worship of God as Lord Shiva; held in spring. Observed all over India.

Pongal or Makar Sankrānti: Worship of God at the time of the winter solstice. Observed in southern and eastern India.

Navarātri: Nine-day worship of God as the Divine Mother; observed in autumn. Observed in northern, central and southern India.

Ganesh Pūjā/Ganesh Chaturthī or Vināyak Chaturthī: Worship of God as the giver of success; observed in early autumn. Observed in western India, particularly the state of Maharashtra.

Ratha Yātrā: Festival during which a symbolic image of God in a chariot is pulled by devotees; held in summer. Observed in eastern India, particularly in the states of Orissa and Bengal.

Holi: Festival celebrating an event of the Divine Incarnation Lord Krishna's life. Along with His worship, devotees throw bright colored liquid and powder at each other; held in spring. Observed in northern and eastern India.

Chhat Pūjā: Worship of God in winter using the Sun as a symbol. Observed in eastern India, particularly in the states of Bihar and Uttar Pradesh.

Bahāg Bihu, Kāti Bihu and Māgh Bihu: Seasonal festivals held respectively in spring, autumn and winter. Observed in northeastern India, particularly in the state of Assam.

Durgā Pūjā: Four-day worship of God as the Divine Mother Durgā; held in autumn. Observed in eastern India, particularly in the state of Bengal.

Kālī Pūjā: Nocturnal worship of God as the Divine Mother Kālī ; held three weeks after Durga Pūjā. Observed in eastern India, particularly in the state of Bengal.

Sarasvatī Pūjā: Worship of God as the Divine Mother Sarasvatī, the bestower of success in education, music and other arts; held in winter. Observed in eastern India, particularly in the state of Bengal.

Shrī Krishna Janmāshtamī: Birthday celebration of the Divine Incarnation Lord Krishna; observed in late summer. Observed all over India.

Rakshā Bandhan: Festival during which sisters put color-ful cotton wrist bands on their brothers as a token of their sisterly love; held in summer. Observed in northern India.

Rām Navamī: Birthday celebration of the Divine Incarnation Lord Rāma; observed in spring in northern India.

Bhrātri Dvitīyā or Bhāi Duj: Festival known as Brother's Day during which sisters pray to God for the long life of their brothers; held in winter. Observed in northern and eastern India and Nepal.

Vaishākhī or Navavarsha: Festival in spring celebrating
the advent of the New Year according to the Indian
Lunar Calendar. Observed in northern and eastern
India.

Lakshmī Pujā: Worship of God as the Divine Mother Lakshmī, the giver of wealth and prosperity; held on
the first full moon day after Durgā Pujā in autumn,
particularly in the state of Bengal.

Appendix C

SUGGESTED READING

Advanced History of India
  R. C. Majumdar, H. C. Raychaudhuri & K. K. Datta

Bhagavad Gita
  Swami Gambhirananda

Bhakti Yoga
  Swami Vivekananda

Essentials of Hinduism
  Swami Vivekananda

The Gospel of Sri Ramakrishna
  Swami Nikhilananda

Hindu View of Life
  S. Radhakrishnan

Hinduism at a Glance
  Swami Nirvedananda

Hinduism
  M. Monier Williams

Hinduism
  R. C. Zaehner

Hinduism: Its Meaning for the Liberation of the Spirit
  Swami Nikhilananda

Indian Philosophy, 2 vols.
  S. Radhakrishnan

Introduction to Indian Philosophy
  S. Chatterjee & D. M. Datta
Jnana Yoga
  Swami Vivekananda
Karma Yoga
  Swami Vivekananda
Mahabharata
  Kamala Subramaniam
Meditation, Mind and Patanjali's Yoga
  Swami Bhaskarananda
Outlines of Indian Philosophy
  M. Hiriyanna
Primer of Hinduism
  D. S. Sarma
Primer of Hinduism
  J. N. Farquhar
Raja Yoga
  Swami Vivekananda
Religion of the Hindus
  K. W. Morgan (ed)
The Upanishads—Breath of the Eternal
  Swami Prabhavananda
Vivekananda, the Yogas and other Works
  Swami Nikhilananda & Frederick Manchester
What is Hinduism?
  D. S. Sarma
The Wonder That Was India
  A. L. Basham
Yoga for Beginners
  Swami Jnaneswarananda

GLOSSARY

Āchārya: A spiritual teacher; also teacher of secular education.

Adroha: Freedom from malice.

Advaita: A school of Vedānta philosophy, teaching the oneness of God, soul and the universe.

Āgama: A class of literature pertaining to Tantra.

Āgāmī Karma: The effects of the deeds of the present life to be experienced in the future; also called Kriyamāna Karma.

Agni: The fire-element.

Agnihotra: A kind of ritualistic worship where fire was used as the symbol of God.

Ahimsā: Nonviolence.

Ajnāna: A term in Vedānta philosophy, meaning ignorance of the Divine Reality. According to the Advaita school of philosophy ajnāna is responsible for man's bondage and suffering in this world.

Ākāsha: The sky-element.

Alolupta: Non-covetousness.

Ānanda: Bliss.

Antevāsin: A student.

Ap: The water-element.

Apaishuna: Refraining from vilification and backbiting.

Aparigraha: Non-acceptance of unnecessary gifts from others.

Ārātrika (Ārati): Ritualistic worship of God by using symbols of the five elements which according to Hinduism constitute this world. Incense, water, light, a hand fan, and a piece of

201

cloth are used as symbols to represent the elements earth, water, fire, air and ether (sky). They are waved in front of the image of the deity.

Ardhāṅginī: (lit., a half body) A wife.

Ārjava: Straightforwardness.

Arjuna: A heroic prince of the *Mahābhārata* who was the son of the king Pāṇḍu and a friend and student of Krishna.

Artha: Wealth, one of the four goals of human life.

Ārya: Indo-Aryan.

Ārya dharma: Religion of the Indo-Aryans.

Ārya Samāj: A reformist Hindu organization started by Swāmī Dayānanda Sarasvatī. See "Dayānanda Sarasvatī."

Āryāvarta: The land of the Indo-Aryans.

Āsana: Sitting posture related to Raja Yoga.

Ātman: The Self; Soul; Indwelling Spirit.

Ātyantika Pralaya: Absolute dissolution of the universe.

Avatāra: Incarnation of God.

Avāntara mukti: Liberation achieved through stages; also known as krama-mukti.

Avidyā: A term of Vedānta philosophy meaning ignorance. See "ajnāna."

Avyakta: The unmanifested state of the universe.

Bhakti Yoga: The Path of Love; one of the four fundamental types of spiritual discipline.

Bhagavad Gītā: A well-known Hindu scripture which forms a part of the epic *Mahābhārata*.

Bhāgavata: One of the Purānas.

Bhūta: (lit., what has come into being) Any of the five elementary constituents of the universe, namely, ākāsha, vāyu, agni, ap and kshiti.

Brahman: Impersonal God; the Absolute Reality.

Brahmā: God as the Creator; the name of the creator aspect of God.

Brahmacharya: The first stage of Hindu life; the stage of studentship. Also means celibacy.

Brahmaloka: The highest plane of existence.

Brahmin: One who belongs to the priestly caste.

Brāhmo Samāj: A theistic organization of India, founded by Rājā Rāmmohan Roy.

Buddha: One of the incarnations of God; also the founder of Buddhism.

Buddhism: A religion which is an offshoot of Hinduism. It is atheistic and sets the goal of spiritual life as complete cessation of misery.

Chandī: A scripture in which the Divine Mother is described as the Ultimate Reality. *Chandī* forms a part of the *Mārkandeya Purāna*.

Chidākāsha: "Knowledge" space.

Chit: Consciousness, knowledge.

Dama: The control of the external organs.

Darshana: Hindu philosophy.

Dashnāmī Order: A monastic order which was started by the great Hindu saint and philosopher Shankarāchārya. See "Shankarāchārya."

Dāsya: The attitude of a devotee expressing the relationship of a servant to God.

Dayānanda Sarasvatī: The founder of the Ārya Samāj (1824–1883).

Deva: (lit., That which shines): A being with a body that gives out light; a god.

Devī: (Feminine form of Deva) A goddess.

Dhāranā: Fixing the mind on a single object.

Dharma: (lit., that which holds up the existence of anything) Essential quality; religion; code of duties; duty.

Dhruva: A saint in Hindu mythology.

Dhyāna: Meditation; the state of uninterrupted concentration of the mind on a single object.

Divine Mother: God looked upon as mother.

Dol Pūrnimā/Holi: The Hindu spring festival associated with Krishna's life.

Durgā: A name of the Divine Mother.

Durgā Pūjā: The worship of Durgā. See *Durgā*.

Dvaita: The philosophy of Dualism; a sub-school of Vedānta.Four stages of Aryan life: Brahmacharya (life of an unmarried student), gārhasthya (life of a married house-holder), vānaprasthya (life of a retired householder), and sannyāsa (life of a monk).

Gafurov, Bobodzhan: A native of Tajikstan, he specialized in the history of Middle Asia and Asia Minor. He was the Director of the Institute of Oriental Studies, Moscow, and a member of the Academy of Sciences of the U.S.S.R.

Gārgī: A great woman scholar of the Vedic period.

Gārhasthya: The second stage of Hindu life; the stage of a family man.

Gāyatrī Mantra: A sacred verse of the *Rig-Veda* recited daily by Hindus of the three upper castes after they have been invested with the sacred thread (Upavīta); also known as Sāvitrī Mantra.

Guna: Property or characteristic trait; any of the three subtle substances which constitute Prakriti or Mother Nature. According to Sānkhya philosophy, Prakriti consists of three gunas known as sattva, rajas, and tamas. Tamas stands for inertia or dullness; rajas for activity or restlessness; sattva for balance, harmony or righteousness.

Guru: Spiritual teacher; also one who gives secular education.

Hatha Yoga: A school of yoga that aims chiefly at physical health and well-being.

Hiranyagarbha: The first created being through whom God projects the physical universe. Also called Brahmā.

Householder: A family man or woman; a person who is not a monastic.

Hrī: Modesty.

Īshvara: God the Creator; Saguna Brahman; Personal God.

Japa: Repetition of a holy name.

Jātyantara Parināma: Transformation of one genus or species into another.

Jīvanmukta: One who has become liberated even while alive.

Jīvanmukti: The state of a jīvanmukta.

Jnāna Yoga: The Path of Knowledge; one of the four fundamental types of spiritual discipline.

Kalki: Name of the last of the ten divine incarnations mentioned in the Purānas.

Kalpa: A periodic cycle of Creation and Dissolution.

Kamalākānta: A saint of Bengal.

Karma: Action, deed, work; result or effect of action.

Karma Yoga: The Path of Right Action; one of the four fundamental types of spiritual discipline.

Karmaphala: (lit., the fruit of an action) The consequences of deeds which come back to the doer in the shape of pain or pleasure. Karmaphala is of three kinds—prārabdha, sanchita and kriyamāna (also called āgāmī).

Krishna: An Incarnation of God.

Kriyamāna: (lit., what is being done) The effect of the deeds of the present life to be experienced in the future.

Kshamā: Forgiveness.

Kshatriya: A person belonging to the military caste.

Kshiti: Earth element.

Kundalinī: The dormant spiritual power of man which resides between the base of the sexual organ and the anus. When awakened through spiritual practice, it enters the sushumnā channel which is inside the backbone and starts coursing upward toward the brain. Inside the sushumnā channel there are six different centers of spiritual awareness called Chakras. They are, in ascending order: (1) Mūlādhāra, (2) Svādhishthāna, (3) Manipura, (4) Anāhata, (5) Vishuddha and (6) Ājnā. These Chakras are visualized by the Yogīs as so many lotuses. The Mūlādhāra Chakra, situated near the anus, is a four-petalled lotus. The Svādhishthāna Chakra, situated at the base of the sexual organ, has six petals. The Manipura Chakra, which is in the region of the navel, is a ten-petaled lotus. The Anāhata Chakra, located in the region of the heart, contains twelve petals. The Vishuddha Chakra, near the base of the throat, has sixteen petals. The Ājnā Chakra, situated in between the two eyebrows, is a two-petaled lotus. Mūlādhāra is the seat of the Kundalinī power. After being awakened, this power passes through these six Chakras and reaches the cerebrum where the Sahasrāra, the thousand petaled lotus is located. The Sahasrāra is the seat of God (Shiva). When the awakened Kundalinī power reaches the Sahasrāra, the spiritual aspirant becomes illumined.

Lakshmī: The Deity who is the giver of wealth and prosperity.

The Purānas mention Lakshmī as the Consort of Lord Vishnu and also as the Goddess of Fortune.

Līlā: Sport; Divine Play.

Madhura: The attitude of a devotee who looks upon God as the Beloved.

Madhvāchārya: A famous Hindu saint and philosopher of South India (1199–1278); also known as Ānandatīrtha; founder of the school of Dualistic Vedānta philosophy (Dvaita Vada).

Mahānirvāna Tantra: A classic Tantric scripture.

Mahātmā Gāndhī: Mohandās Karamchānd Gāndhī; well known political leader of India renowned for his nonviolent political movement; considered by many Indians as the father of the nation.

Mahāvākya(s): Important sentences in the *Vedas* which speak of the divinity of man and the nature of God.

Mānava Dharma: Religion of Man; one of the several names of the religion of the Indo-Aryans.

Mantra: A sacred formula to be uttered in connection with rituals; also a set of holy words.

Mārdava: Gentleness.

Mārga: Path.

Māyā: God's power of creating illusions.

Meerā Bāi: A great medieval woman saint of North India (1504–1550).

Moksha: Liberation from all kinds of bondage; liberation attained through spiritual enlightenment.

Mukti: Same as moksha.

Naimittika Pralaya: Cyclic Cosmic Dissolution during Hiranya-garbha's sleep.

Nāta-mandira: The audience hall in a Hindu temple.

Nididhyāsana: Deep concentration on Self-Knowledge.

Nigama: A class of literature pertaining to Tantra.

Nirguna Brahman: Impersonal God; God without any attributes.

Nirvikalpa Samādhi: A super-conscious state during which the aspirant realizes his absolute oneness with the Universal Spirit or Nirguna Brahman.

Nivritti Mārga: The path of renunciation of sensual desires.

Nrisimha: (lit., Man-lion) A Divine Incarnation mentioned in the Purānas.

Nyāya: Indian Logic; one of the six systems of Hindu philosophy.

Om: The most sacred word of the *Vedas*, also written as Aum. It is a symbol of God.

Pancha rina: Five debts.

Panchīkarana: (lit. quintupling) According to the Vedānta school a particular process by which the five elements constituting the universe are said to be compounded with one another to form this universe.

Pānini: A famous grammarian of ancient India.

Pārvatī: Another name of Shakti.

Patanjali: Founder of the Yoga system of Hindu philosophy.

Pathyasvatī: A great woman scholar of the Vedic period.

Pingalā: A nerve channel in the spinal column.

Prahlāda: A great devotee of Vishnu whose life is mentioned in the Purānas.

Prakriti: Primordial Nature, which in association with Purusha creates the universe. It is one of the categories of the Sānkhya school of philosophy.

Prākrita Pralaya: Cosmic Dissolution at the end of Hiranyagarbha's life span, when he becomes liberated.

Pralaya: Cosmic Dissolution.

Prāṇāyāma: A kind of breathing exercise helpful in gaining mental concentration.

Pranava: The holy syllable Om of Hinduism.

Prārabdha: The karmic force that determines one's present life.

Prasāda: Food or drink that has been offered to the Deity.

Pratyāhāra: The process of withdrawing one's mind from sense objects.

Pravritti Mārga: The Path of Permitted Sensual Desires, suitable for householders.

Prithivī: The earth element, also called *kshiti*.

Purāna(s): Hindu mythology.

Purī Order: One of the branches of the Dashnāmī monastic order founded by Shankarāchārya.

Purusha: (lit., a man) A term of the Sānkhya philosophy, denoting the eternal Sentient Principle; according to Sānkhya, there are many Purushas.

Pūrva Mimāmsā: One of the six major systems of Hindu philosophy.

Rajas: One of the three subtle substances constituting Prakriti or Mother Nature.

Rāja Yoga: The Path of Mental Concentration; one of the four fundamental types of spiritual discipline.

Rāma: A Divine Incarnation; the epic *Rāmāyana* is the story of his life.

Rāmakrishna: A 19th century Hindu saint (1836–1886) known as the saint of the harmony of religions; also regarded as a Divine Incarnation by many.

Rāmānujāchārya: A famous saint and philosopher of South India, the founder of the school of Qualified Nondualism (Vishishtādvaita Vāda).

Rāmāyana: A famous Hindu epic authored by Vālmīki.

Rāmprasād: A well-known saint of Bengal; composer of many songs about the Divine Mother (1723–1803).

Rishi: Seer of God, sage.

Rita: Eternal moral order.

Saguna Brahman: Brahman with attributes; Impersonal God seen through māyā as Personal God; the Creator, Preserver, and Destroyer of the universe.

Sahadharminī: A wife.

Sahasrāra: The thousand-petalled lotus in the cerebrum. See *Kundalinī.*

Sakhya: The attitude of a devotee who looks upon God as a friend.

Samādhi: Mental concentration par excellence.

Samhitā: One of the two primary sections of each of the Vedas containing hymns and sacred formulas (mantras).

Sanātana Dharma: (lit., the eternal religion) One of the names of the religion of the Indo-Aryans.

Sannyāsa: The 4th stage of Hindu life; the stage of complete renunciation.

Sannyāsin: An all-renouncing monk, who belongs to the fourth stage of Hindu life.

Satchidānanda: The ocean of Existence, Knowledge and Bliss; a metaphorical expression suggesting the indescribable Absolute Reality or Nirguna Brahman.

Savikalpa Samādhi: A kind of Samādhi in which one retains a trace of one's ego. See *Samādhi.*

Sāvitrī Mantra: See *Gāyatrī Mantra.*

Shaiva: A Hindu sect worshiping God as Shiva.

Shaiva Āgama(s): A class of scriptural texts of the Shaiva sect.

Shākta: A Hindu sect worshiping God as the Divine Mother; a member of this sect; pertaining to this sect.

Shankarāchārya: The great saint and Vedantist philosopher of South India (c.700–740).

Shānta: The unemotional attitude of a devotee contemplating the infinite glories of Personal God.

Shānti: Peace.

Shaucha: Purification of body and mind.

Shiva: The Destroyer aspect of God.

Shraddhā: Implicit faith in one's teacher or other respected people.

Shrīmad Bhāgavata: One of the Purānas.

Shruti: (lit., anything heard) Revealed knowledge; the Vedas.

Shūdra: One who belongs to the caste of farmers, artisans, etc.

Siddhi(s): Supernatural power(s).

Smriti(s): (lit., anything remembered) Any scripture other than the Vedas, especially one laying down social and domestic laws.

Snātaka: A student who has completed his education.

Srishti: Creation.

Sthiti: Continued existence—the state of the universe during the interval between Creation and Dissolution.

Sthūla: Gross; physical, as opposed to subtle (sūkshma).

Sūkshma: Fine; subtle.

Tamas: One of the three subtle substances constituting Prakriti or Mother Nature.

Tanmātra(s): The elementary constituents of the universe.

Tantra: A class of scriptural texts, not derived directly from the Vedas, presenting God as Shiva and Shakti.

Upanishad(s): Scriptures, very rich in philosophical content, which form a part of the Vedas.

Upāsanā: Worship of God.

Vaishnava: A Hindu sect worshiping God as Vishnu.

Vaishya: One who belongs to the traders' caste.

Vānaprasthya: The third stage of Aryan life; the stage of a retired person.

Vārānasī: One of the holiest cities of India.

Vātsalya: The attitude of a devotee expressing a parental relationship with God, looking upon Him as a child.

Vāyu: Air element.

Vedānta: (lit., the end of the Vedas) The Upanishads; also one of the six systems of Hindu philosophy.

Vidyāsāgar, Īshvar Chandra: A great educator, reformer and philanthropist of Bengal (1820–1891).

Vīja Mantra(s): The sacred syllable(s), signifying God.

Virāt: The presiding Deity of the physical universe.

Vishistādvaita (Qualified Nondualism): A sub-school of Vedānta philosophy founded by Rāmānuja, according to which the soul and nature are the modes of Brahman, and the individual soul is part of Brahman.

Vishwāmitra: Sage to whom the Gāyatrī Mantra was revealed.

Vishnu: The Preserver aspect of God.

Vivekānanda, Swāmī: Renowned Hindu monk; founder of the Rāmakrishna Order of monks and the Rāmakrishna Mission; first effective preacher of Hinduism in the West (1863–1902).

Vyāsa: Also known as Vādarāyana. The great sage of the Vedic period; the compiler of the Vedas, and the author of the

Brahma Sutras and the Hindu epic *Mahābhārata*.

Yama: A preliminary course of moral discipline prescribed in Rāja Yoga.

Yoga: (lit., union with God); any course of spiritual discipline that makes for such union.

Yogī: One who practices Yoga.

INDEX

Santosha (contentment), 99
Sāradā Devī, Shrī, 85
Sarasvatī, 73
Sarasvatī, Swāmī Dayānanda, 54
Sārdā Act, 45*n*
Sat-Chid-Ānandam, 68
Sattva, 159
    characteristics in *Bhagavad Gītā*, 163
    characteristics of, 161
    -guna gives spiritual liberation, 163
    parable of robbers, 163–164
    preponderance of, 162
    (*see* Guna)
Satya (truthfulness in thought and deed), 99
Satyakāma, 105–106
Savikalpa Samādhi, 122
Sāvitrī Mantra
    (*see* Gāyatrī)
Sāvitrī, 52
Schopenhauer, Arthur, 193
Scriptures, 3, 5
    of Shākta sect, 62
    of Vaishnava and Shaiva sects, 62
    (*see Bhagavad Gītā, Bhāgavata Purāna, Chandī, Mahābhārata*, Pancharātra Samhitās, Purānas, *Rāmāyana*, Samhitā and Brāhmana, *Shaiva Āgamas*, Smritis, Tantra literature, Upanishads, Vedas)
Sects, or denominations, 38
Seers, 12
Self-effort, 87
Self-sacrifice, 58
Sense organs, 92
Shaiva Āgamas, 20

(*see* Tantra)
Shaiva, 62
Shakti
    dialogues of, 20
    God as Female principle, 19
Shāndilya, 23
Shāndilya-vidyā, 182
Shankara, 18, 38
    analogy of the rope, 177
    meaning of the word *real*, 176
    refutation of objection to many theories of creation, 176
    rope represents Nirguna Brahman, 177
Shankarāchārya
    (*see* Shankara)
Shānta (serene and dispassionate attitude), 118
Shānti (peace of mind attained by control of mind), 99
Shaucha (purification of body and mind), 99
Shiva
    dialogues of, 20
    God looked upon as Male principle, 19
    Ishvara's destroyer aspect, 71
Shraddhā
    for the guru, 105, 106
Shrāddha, ceremony, 40
Shravana, 121
    (*see* Jnāna Yoga)
Shruti, 11
Shūdra(s), 24
    lowest caste, 26
    (*see* Castes)
Shvetāshvatara Upanishad, 15
Siddha mantra, 147
Siddhis, 126–127

Vyakti-dharma (dharma of an
individual), 98–99
(*see* Dharma)
Vyāsa, 12, 12*n*
school founded by, 17

W

Widows, remarriage of, 35
Women, condition of, 52–58
Worship (pūja or upāsanā)
and adoration of God, 117
external ritualistic, 117,
139–141
and fasting, 140
of God, 137–143
of God through images,
137–138
mental, 117, 139
quotation from Shrī
Rāmakrishna on, 191
using symbols of the five
elements, 140
using yantras as symbols of
God in Tantra, 150
Worshiper, 140

Y

Yājnavalkya, 17, 98
a dialogue with Maitreyī,
98
Yajur-Veda, 12, 185
Yama, 122
Yantra(s)
are holy diagrams, 150
mantras and 149–150
symbols of God in Tāntrika
worship, 150
Yoga, school, 17
Yogas, four, 115

Z

Zoroastrianism, 1

About the author

A senior monk of the well-known Ramakrishna Order of India which he joined in 1958, Swami Bhaskarananda is the President of the Vedanta Society of Western Washington in Seattle. Since his arrival in America in 1974 the Swami has frequently given talks on Hinduism in churches, synagogues, schools, colleges and universities all over North America. He has also lectured on invitation, in Argentina, Brazil, Uruguay, France, the Netherlands, England, Iceland, Japan and several other Asian countries. He is actively involved in the interfaith movement in America and is a past President of the Interfaith Council of Washington. The Swami is the author of the books *Meditation, Mind and Patanjali's Yoga* and *Life in Indian Monasteries,* and is the founder and editor-in-chief of the quarterly journal *Global Vedanta.* In addition to his duties in Seattle, the Swami is also the spiritual guide of the Vivekananda Vedanta Society of British Columbia in Canada and of the Vedanta Society of Hawaii.

More appreciations of *The Essentials of Hinduism*

"Never before have I read a book on Hinduism like this, which has discussed all the facets of Hinduism so clearly."

—Swami Swananda
Ex-Editor of the *Prabuddha Bharata,*
and retired head of the Vedanta Society of Berkeley, U.S.A.

"Hinduism is one of humanity's most ancient religions and, over time, it has evolved in an incredibly rich but complex form. Its metaphysics and philosophies are especially difficult for people coming from the so-called western religious traditions to grasp. Fortunately for us, Swami Bhaskarananda has come to our aid. His book elucidates Hinduism's essentials in a clearly written manner, with a text that is laced with wonderfully expressive analogies and delightful stories."

—Rabbi Anson Laytner
Past President, Interfaith Council of Washington State

"*The Essentials of Hinduism* is a clear and comprehensive presentation of the Hindu religious tradition. It would have been most beneficial to me had it been available as I went through high school and university studies in Philadelphia and Princeton."

—Dr. Mithra Sankrithi
Boeing Commercial Airplane Group

"*The Essentials of Hinduism* by Swami Bhaskarananda should clear up any misconceptions Westerners might have about the ancient and complex religion of Hinduism. Swami Bhaskarananda goes right to the heart of the difficult subject matter and offers clear and concise explanations. All aspects of Hinduism are covered in this comprehensive work which would be suitable for study at the secondary or college level. Also, a must for the religious collection at the public library."

—Maryte Racys
Librarian, Seattle, Washington, U.S.A.

"...beautifully clear and concise. The best exposition that we have ever seen on the subject."

—Dr. D.E. Longden
Pain specialist, England

Also by Swami Bhaskarananda

Meditation, Mind and Patanjali's Yoga—A Practical Guide to Spiritual Growth for Everyone

A comprehensive and engaging book on meditation and other spiritual practices, with special reference to Patanjali. Discusses genuine spiritual teachers, meditation techniques, Japa, overcoming spiritual obstacles, judging one's own spiritual progress, Yoga, Samkhya philosophy, the stages of spiritual growth and levels of illumination, and removing stress.

"In short, this volume should be useful for both new and accustomed practitioners."

—Library Journal

"...provides a clear, interesting, and comprehensive survey of the Yoga system, from ethics to meditation....It has been a pleasure and inspiration to read this book!"

—Christopher Key Chapple
Professor of Theological Studies
Director of Asian and Pacific Studies
Loyola Marymount University, Los Angeles, CA

"The manuscript is wonderful. Very clear and very very well presented. I thoroughly enjoyed it."

—Prof. John Grimes
Dept. of Religious Studies
Michigan State University